My Buffalo Nickel
and Other Stories From a
Portuguese American Life:
The Life and Writings of
Joseph George Ray

Marie Ray Fraley

Jan-Carol Publishing, Inc

"every story needs a book"

My Buffalo Nickel and Other Stories
From a Portuguese American Life:
The Life and Writings of Joseph George Ray
Marie Ray Fraley

Published September 2023
Heirloom Editions
Imprint of Jan-Carol Publishing, Inc.
All rights reserved
Copyright © 2023 Marie Ray Fraley
Front Cover Design: Jennifer Fraley
Interior Book Design: Tara Sizemore

This book may not be reproduced in whole or part, in any manner whatsoever without written permission, with the exception of brief quotations within book reviews or articles.

The net proceeds of any book sales will be donated to the Institute for Portuguese and Lusophone World Studies at Rhode Island College in Providence, RI.

ISBN: 978-1-962561-02-0
Library of Congress Control Number: 2023946928

Jan-Carol Publishing, Inc.
PO Box 701
Johnson City, TN 37605
publisher@jancarolpublishing.com
www.jancarolpublishing.com

Indulge in me, as it's obvious to see,
I'm an amateur writer of kind.
I submit these offerings of my past,
Arranged in some sort of rhyme.

Excuse if you see, should there be,
Errors in grammar or spelling.
More important is the story, don't you agree,
Of experiences of my past worth telling.

For should I dare to wait too long,
When memory challenges my trust,
It will be too late to record my past,
So to write it all now, I must.

God and I both know what I mean,
and in my passing, now only God knows.

– Joseph "George" Ray

To my father, Joseph "George" Ray,
who not only gave me life, but who, through his love and example,
gave me a life of worth.

Contents

Foreword ix
Preface xi
Introduction xiii
Part One: Early Life 1
Part Two: Military Service 51
Part Three: Family 81
Part Four: The Lace Trade 121
Part Five: Politics And Community Service 137
Part Six: Musings 151
Afterword 175
Addenda 179
    Tributes, Letters, and Notes 179
    Military Profile 187
    Contributions Published in *The Kent County Daily Times* 189
Endnotes 191
References 195
Acknowledgments 197
About the Author 199

FOREWORD

By Sílvia A. Oliveira, Ph.D.
*Associate Professor of Portuguese and Director of the Institute for Portuguese
and Lusophone World Studies, Rhode Island College*

My *Buffalo Nickel* is a captivating book of life writing penned by the editor-author Marie Ray Fraley and by the subject-author, Joseph "George" Ray. In other words, it is an autobiography of a father written by his daughter featuring the father's own words. It is collaborative writing, if posthumous, in that the editor and the subject are of one mind in the desire to "preserve the work of a much loved and appreciated man" who put many of his experiences in writing for the benefit of his grandsons, family, and his community.

It is a multi-genre work of memoir, poetry, published editorial writing, sketching, and photography that takes us on a life journey beginning in 1892, when his Azorean Portuguese grandparents immigrated to the United States, through 2012 when Joseph "George" Ray died at the age of 88 years.

My Buffalo Nickel and Other Stories From a Portuguese American Life sheds light on times, places, and people spanning the twentieth century in the United States during the Depression and World War II. The stories feature Rhode Island and the lace industry that employed many of the Ray brothers; and they speak of and for an ethnic group, the Portuguese, who by the end of the twentieth century made up ten percent of the multicultural heritage in Rhode Island.

I was a newcomer to the Ocean State in 2012 when Marie Fraley's father, Joseph G. Ray, passed away. I was also Marie's colleague at the Institute for Portuguese and Lusophone World Studies, which she helped start at Rhode Island College in 2006 and directed until 2018. From Marie I heard stories about the melting-pot generations of her grandparents and parents, some of them included in this book; and I witnessed her work of advocacy for the Portuguese and Lusophone ethnic heritages of Rhode Island. Her advocacy included co-organizing an international conference on the acculturation and integration of Portuguese immigrants and their descendants; directing an oral history video production documenting the public service of Luso-Americans in Rhode Island; researching and writing on Portuguese American political incorporation in Rhode Island; and organizing countless events of regional, national, and international reach.

Marie's voice in this book seamlessly weaves the elegant and skillful researcher and the devoted daughter. That she accomplished all the above—and this book—after she retired (much like her father did with his memoirs) only confirms that Marie is her father's daughter, and that this is their book.

By Paul J. Tavares
Former General Treasurer of the State of Rhode Island (1999–2007)

It is said in this writing that Joseph "George" Ray was an extraordinary man who lived an ordinary life. It was also said that he was a modern-day Renaissance Man. Both statements are true.

Mr. Ray exemplified what it was to be a member of the greatest generation. He cherished above all else family, country, and his faith. He served his nation in time of war and was dedicated to providing for his family. During his lifetime he experienced both times of austerity and times of abundance. He faced challenges and overcame obstacles.

Although limited in formal education, his natural intelligence, talents, keen insight, and determination led him to have a successful professional career and success in his many other endeavors.

As a son of immigrants, he recognized the challenges and sacrifices of his parents who came to the United States not only to better their lives, but to provide opportunity for a better future for their children. Joseph "George" Ray paid homage to his parents by seizing and making the best of that opportunity. As the case with so many Portuguese-Americans who settled in Rhode Island, this is a responsibility to which many of us can relate.

One cannot come away from reading this well-written biography without having complete admiration for Joseph "George" Ray and the life he lived. This truly is the story of an extraordinary man and a story well worth reading.

Preface

The idea for this book began with the simple intention to preserve the work of a much loved and appreciated man. In his retirement, the weight of my father's memories and musings spilled out of him and found expression in poems, stories, anecdotes, and thoughts jotted down. A self-educated man who was not allowed to finish the tenth grade, his writings were often clever and amusing, although sometimes a bit awkward and unpolished, but they were always honest attempts to reveal life as he experienced it.

Realizing the effort behind that work and the love from which it sprang has compelled me to honor it and preserve it by putting it in print. Easily done—a collection of his works with some well-chosen photos and it's done? Not so fast. While his work could easily stand on its own, there seemed to be so much more to tell about him.

I know too well that Joseph George Ray never gave half measures. He was "all in" with whatever he tackled until he had wrung the absolute best out of it. It seems to me that if this book is to honor him the way he deserves, it should be more than a collection of his written work. It should put that work into the context of the experiences of the life he lived.

This puts me at a great disadvantage, because I did not know the whole man. I did not enter his life until 1950 when he was twenty-six years old and had already seen the suffering and destruction of World War II. Then, for the next forty-five years or so, I knew him only through one lens, as a daughter sees a loving father. He was the provider, the caretaker, the protector, the teacher, the gatekeeper, and the most loving father for whom any girl could wish. Like all normal growth curves, he ran the gamut from my idol and my hero in my childhood, to the man who didn't understand anything and was ruining my life in my adolescence and young adulthood, to the wisest man on earth in my maturity and own parenthood. Amazing how he grew over the years!

In truth, I did not begin to know him as a man with hopes, dreams, struggles, and frustrations until he began to write and to share those thoughts with me. As a self-educated man, he worked hard to put his thoughts on paper, sometimes doubting his ability to do so. As he had given me the formal education that he never enjoyed, he looked to me for feedback and editing. It was the beginning of truly opening up about his childhood memories and certainly it was the first time he spoke of his war experiences. I am grateful that he shared them with me.

Throughout his life, in his work as a lace weaver, rising to management in quality control, in his union activities, politics, even in his volunteer work at the church and in the community, he did his very best to solve whatever problem was before him in order to secure the best result. "If it was worth doing, it was worth doing right," was one of his mottos.

My primary goal in writing his biography is to preserve his work in print in order to share it with his family as well as to create a legacy of a life well lived. Most importantly, it is to honor the life of the man represented by those works and to thank him for the values, the opportunities, and the wonderful life that he has given me. I hope that I am up to the task.

INTRODUCTION

My father was not a simple man. Although he would be the first to tell you in all sincerity that he was, an examination of his life, through his writings and his actions, would argue to the contrary. He was an extraordinary man who lived an ordinary life during a time period of unprecedented extremes from hardship and atrocities to comfort and amazing technological advances. As I am writing this, he is whispering in my ear quoting Charles Dickens from *A Tale of Two Cities*: "It was the best of times, it was the worst of times..." The point is that he managed it all with the unwavering belief that any problem could be solved and any obstacle overcome with the right combination of information, ingenuity, and good old-fashioned hard work.

Joseph "George" Ray was born in 1924 and died in 2012 spanning a lifetime of 88 years. At the time of his birth, President Calvin Coolidge made the first radio address to the nation from the White House, a first class postage stamp was two cents, a Model-T Ford touring car was $295 and Charles Lindberg had yet to cross the Atlantic in a solo flight from New York to Paris in 1927. By the time of his death, he had lived through the Great Depression, landed on Omaha Beach in Normandy during World War II, witnessed men landing on the moon, and could bring up any type of information on a smart phone no larger than the palm of one's hand.

He would never say that he handled his challenges any better than anyone else of "the greatest generation." He was the middle child in a family of Portuguese Azorean immigrants in a small New England textile town that drew poor yet hopeful Europeans traveling in steerage on trans-Atlantic steamers from the Azores, Poland, Italy, Greece, and Ireland joining the Quebecois from Canada. He suffered discrimination and mockery growing up, uncertain employment in a dying lace manufacturing trade, and devastating deterioration from progressive Parkinson's Disease later in life. Through his verbal stories, writings, and my personal observations, I saw in him great faith, courage, and silent strength at times when many would have given up. I can say unashamedly that he was my hero.

The story of his life is more than a collection of writings, a biographical outline of dates and facts, or even a series of anecdotes of what happened when. His story is a journey that we will take together along a road of many twists, turns, detours and, perhaps, the occasional "road not taken" (he's saying quote Robert Frost here). I am taking this journey with you, the reader, as I rediscover his many poems, recollections, and the clippings and notes that he drew upon for inspiration as this tapestry of his life was woven. Along the way are times of simple joy and wonder but also confusion, frustration, and worry. This is his journey being told. At times I am the observer and at others, a participant, but will be forever grateful for having been along with him for some of the ride.

Part One:
Early Life

"WHAT'S IN A NAME?"

The name that a person carries through life should be a simple enough thing. Parents choose a name for their child based on family tradition or just to suit their own tastes or whim. It goes on a birth certificate and, aside from the family nicknames or "endearments," it sticks for a lifetime and is the official proof of identity in all civil matters, such as school registration, passport application, or military service—perhaps?

This was not the case for the son of Frank and Mary Ray. In the 1920s, babies were born at home requiring registration at the local town or city hall. Indeed, this child was registered in the town of West Warwick, Rhode Island as "Joseph Ray" on February 4, 1922, son of Frank Ray and Mary Ferris according to an official stamped delayed birth certificate[i] issued by the State of Rhode Island. Church records, however, do not agree.

European immigrants at that time, Azorean Portuguese included, were largely Roman Catholic. Babies were baptized as soon as possible after their birth to ensure that their immortal souls would go directly to heaven avoiding the fate of eternal limbo should there be an untimely infant death. With infant mortality rates so high at that time, this was not an unfounded fear. Baptisms took place at least within two weeks of birth, if not within days. Mothers customarily did not even attend the baptisms still recovering from childbirth and too weak to leave the house. The reliance on baptismal records posted so close to the date of birth became the accepted primary document of proof. In fact, church records included date and place of birth as well as that of the sacrament of Baptism.

Born on the 29th of January in 1924, the third child of Frank and Mary Ray was baptized on the following 3rd of February in Saints Peter and Paul Church in the village of Lippitt, Rhode Island—only five days after his birth. The record shows date and place of birth, the names of the parents and godparents but most importantly his name, GEORGIUS. Curiously enough, all names were written in Latin in the records of this church at that time; however, it is clear that he was named GEORGE, not Joseph. That his birth was registered the next day at the West Warwick Town Hall as "Joseph Ray" is a mystery assuming that it was his parents' intention that he be named "George." It would also be assumed that Frank Ray would take charge of the registration of his son at the West Warwick Town Hall presenting the baptism certificate from the day before.

Indeed, throughout his life he was called "George" at school and by everyone who knew him and "Georgie" by his family. A tattered First Holy Communion certificate from St. Anthony's Church dated the 14th of June 1931 shows his name as *"Jorge Rei."* The Portuguese priest, Father Vincent, used the Portuguese equivalents of both his first name, *Jorge* for George, and his last name, *Rei* for the anglicized Ray. (More about this later.) A school certificate attesting to his promotion from the ninth grade of West Warwick Junior High School also shows him to be "George Ray."

All was certainly straightforward until "George" enlisted in the U.S. Army during World War II. His draft registration card shows that he registered under the name of "George Ray" with correct date of birth and address; however, when he returned to the draft board, he was told, "Your name is Joseph, not George!" He said that he did not question it and that the officer did not further explain the basis for the change. The digitized copy of his draft registration card indeed shows the name "George" crossed out with "Joseph" written above it.[ii] From that point forward, he was "Joseph Ray" in the military. Upon returning home, he adopted "Joseph George Ray" and "Joseph G. Ray" to avoid confusion. In spite of many inquiries, I have been unable to discover the basis upon which the military changed his name from "George" to "Joseph." One can only assume that the military's research into his birth registration at West Warwick Town Hall or State of Rhode Island Department of Vital Statistics, showed him to be "Joseph."

Part One: Early Life

U.S., World War II Draft Cards Young Men, 1940-1947 for Joseph Ray
Rhode Island > Miranda-Silva > Ragosta, Carmine-Raymond, Alberic

REGISTRATION CARD—(Men born on or after January 1, 1922 and on or before June 30, 1924)

SERIAL NUMBER: N 613
1. NAME (Print): Joseph Ray
ORDER NUMBER: 12624
2. PLACE OF RESIDENCE (Print): 60 Wakefield St, West Warwick, Kent, R.I.
3. MAILING ADDRESS: Same
4. TELEPHONE: None
5. AGE IN YEARS: 18
6. PLACE OF BIRTH: West Warwick, Kent, R.I.
DATE OF BIRTH: Jan 09 1924
7. NAME AND ADDRESS OF PERSON WHO WILL ALWAYS KNOW YOUR ADDRESS: Frank Joseph Ray - 60 Wakefield St, West War, R.I.
8. EMPLOYER'S NAME AND ADDRESS: Crompton - Richmond Co. - Crompton, R.I.
9. PLACE OF EMPLOYMENT OR BUSINESS: Crompton, West Warwick, Kent, R.I.

D. S. S. Form 1 (Revised 6-1-42)
(Signature): Joseph Ray

The saga of the family's name change began well before the birth of George Ray. The son of Azorean Portuguese immigrants, the family surname underwent alterations as well. In 1892, his grandfather, *Francisco Furtado REI*, made a solo transatlantic voyage from *Ponta Delgada*, island of *São Miguel* in the Azores followed by his wife, *Antónia dos Santos Correia* with sons, *Francisco* and *Manuel*, the following year in 1893. For some unknown reason, *Antónia* returned to *São Miguel* in 1894 or 1895 alone with the boys and a daughter, *Maria*, who had been born in the United States. She came back to the United States arriving aboard the *"Olinda"* in Boston on April 3, 1895 to meet her husband, "*F. F. REY*" according to the ship's manifest.

The variation in spelling in the surname between "*Rei*" and "*Rey*" is not significant because "*Rey*" is considered to be an "old Portuguese" spelling actually derived from Spanish Galician.[iii] It is possible that, given the Spanish derivation of the name, our Portuguese ancestors could have been Sephardic Jews, who escaped from Spain to Portugal during the Spanish Inquisition of 1492 under the regime of Ferdinand and Isabella of Spain.

How *Rei*, even *Rey*, became Ray in the United States is an interesting story. It certainly was not changed by customs officers at Ellis Island or even Boston which is a common myth. The name with which one left the port of departure on a ship's manifest was clearly the name with which one was checked against and gained legal entry into the United States. Moreover, in order to apply for United States citizenship later, one applied under the name with which they arrived showing proof of legal entry on that same ship's manifest in order for that application to proceed.

When my grandfather *Francisco Rei*, son of *Francisco Furtado Rei* and *Antónia dos Santos Correia*, was registered for school at the age of six, the family was asked to state his name. "*Francisco Rei*." "How do you spell it?" Unable to spell it in English and with no document, it sounded like "Ray," and that is what was entered—or so the family story goes. Indeed, *Francisco Rei* went by Frank Ray all his life. It was not only simpler and easier to assimilate into American society but suited his personal desire to become an American. He certainly was able to pass as one because he was fair skinned with light eyes, like his mother *Antónia*, and spoke English without an accent having been educated in American schools from an early age.

As mentioned previously, when he submitted his Declaration of Intention for U.S. citizenship in 1932, Frank Ray was required to apply under the name of *Francisco Rei* to match the ship's manifest to prove legal entry. By 1935, when his petition had been accepted and he appeared in court to swear his oath of allegiance, the judge made note of his customary use of the name "Frank Ray." The family story is told that the judge said to Frank, "Mr. Ray, I notice that you typically use the name Frank Ray. If you wish to legally change your name from *Francisco Rei* to Frank Ray, you may do so now." Agreeing to the suggestion, the name change to Frank Joseph Ray was made official and legal by court order from June 1, 1935 forward.

SON OF IMMIGRANTS

George was the third son and the middle child of five children born to *Francisco Rei / Frank Joseph Ray* and *Maria dos Anjos de Faria / Mary Ferris*, who were married at Our Lady of the Rosary Church in Fox Point, Providence, on April 16, 1917. The family constellation consisted of Francis Joseph (1918), Alfred Joseph (1922), Joseph George (1924), Thomas Anthony (1929), and Evelyn Marie (1931), all born in Rhode Island. Both Frank and Mary immigrated aboard steamer ships as children with their parents departing from the port of *Ponta Delgada* on the island of *São Miguel* and arriving in Boston or New Bedford in the mid-1890s to early 1900s.

Frank was the second born but first surviving son of *Francisco Furtado Rei* and *Antónia dos Santos Correia* of the *freguesia* (village) of *Ribeira das Tainhas*, thereby taking on all the characteristics of the eldest child. Mary was also the second born but the eldest surviving child and daughter of *José Jacintho de Faria* and *Maria dos Anjos Pimentel* of the *freguesia* (village) of *Rabo de Peixe*.

By all indications, the families were laborers or tenant farmers living under poverty conditions on the island. Uprooting the family to seek better opportunities in the "land of milk and honey," like thousands of other European immigrants at the turn of the 20th century, was not an uncommon occurrence. Indeed, Mary was old enough to remember living in a small hovel with dirt floors before leaving *Rabo de Peixe* at eight years of age. They banked everything on this chance to improve their lot as families typically sold all their furniture and belongings to raise the funds for the transatlantic passage in steerage.

Both the *Rei* and the *de Faria* families settled in the western section of Warwick (later incorporated as the town of West Warwick in 1913) drawn to the jobs in the many textile mills dotted along the Pawtuxet

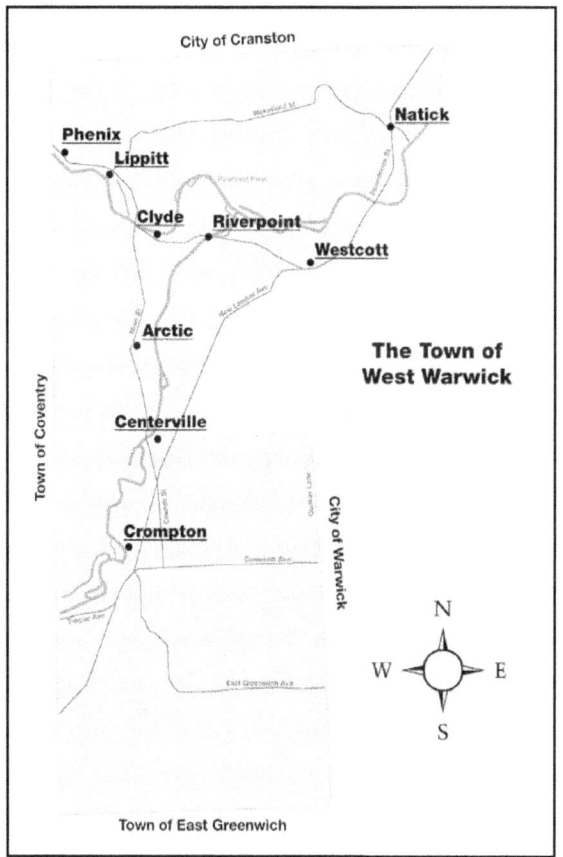

Source: http://www.milltowndocumentary.org/villages/

River running through the town. Azorean Portuguese immigrants largely settled in the villages of Phenix, Lippitt, Clyde, and River Point which gave rise to the establishment of a national Portuguese language Roman Catholic Church, St. Anthony's, on Maple Avenue in River Point in 1925.

The same scenario was repeated throughout the town with the Polish settling in Compton, the Italians settling in Natick, and the French Canadians in the village of Arctic. The Irish and the English were already well established at the turn of the century and, like the cream, rose to the top of the town hierarchy for jobs and opportunities with their command of the English language. As George recounts it:

> *"...the ensuing years were less pleasant for surrounding immigrant children where the pecking order was established by Irish and French children. They held the privileges of their dominion with guarded jealousy harassing and tormenting the immigrants who entered their turf. Difficult as it was, my dad and others persevered."*

George's father, Frank Ray, was an intelligent and clever individual who sought and capitalized upon opportunities in his new country. Frank's account of his assimilation into American culture, as told to George, continues:

> *"Within three years of his arrival, my dad became fluent in English. So much so, many Portuguese immigrants would solicit his help in interpreting for them when the need arose. Leaving school at the age of nine, he applied for a job in a textile mill where cheap child labor was sought after by the mill barons. Illegal as it was to hire children, they worked twelve hours a day for pennies an hour. When labor officials visited the premises, the children were rushed up into the bell tower to escape detection.*
>
> *"With the passing of time at age thirteen, he worked weekends in a barbershop as an apprentice sweeping floors. There were many Canadian French-speaking customers who frequented the shop. It wasn't long before Dad could converse in French with some degree of acceptance continuing to improve in his third language with the passing of time.*
>
> *"By the age of sixteen, Dad was earning $6.50 for a sixty hour week as an assistant foreman in a (textile) printworks. In addition, due to a fondness for horses, he and his cousin Manuel exercised and cared for Mr. Knight's thoroughbreds becoming himself an*

expert horseman through the process. Mr. Knight was the owner of B. B. & R. Knight, one of the largest textile mills in the state.

"Never content and always eager to succeed, my dad delivered newspapers for a Mr. Rose with a horse and buggy that took the better part of a Sunday morning. In return, along with his stipend, he was allowed to saddle ride some of Mr. Rose's horses. Mr. Rose was an entrepreneur that Dad befriended and with whom he enjoyed a long association. Mom tells me that Dad was a very attractive man and that he took pleasure in riding Mr. Rose's horses at full gallop through the village streets impressing many of the young single ladies, Mom included.

"As years passed, Dad took up the slide trombone and became a fine concert soloist. During the silent movie era, Dad was an accompanist in the pit orchestra of the Thornton Theatre where we kids were allowed free admission on occasion due to Dad's position. Music became an important financial contributor to our family. During the Great Depression which started in this region around 1927, Dad took on jobs with parade and concert bands as well as in silent movie and vaudeville theaters. To further augment his income, he gave trombone lessons to a number of students in the front parlor on Sundays charging fifty cents for a half hour session."

In later years, through my genealogical research, it was discovered that the *Correia* line of the family through Frank's mother, *Antónia dos Santos*, were talented in the making and playing of the twelve-string Azorean guitar, the viola, in *Ribeira das Tainhas*. In fact, the family was known by "Viola" and answered to that *"alcunha"* or nickname.[iv] This musical talent found expression in Frank and his brothers and sister. Besides Frank on the trombone, Manuel played the tuba, "Tony" played the saxophone and clarinet, Josephine played some piano, John played the banjo and the guitar, and tried the trumpet and string bass. Most accomplished of them was "Joe" who studied clarinet and saxophone at the Boston Conservatory of Music, played in orchestras, gave lessons and tuned pianos for a living.[v]

The Frank and Mary Ray family settled in a small house on Wakefield Street up the hill from the Lippitt Mill among English, Irish and French Canadian families rather than with other Portuguese-Americans near the bottom of the hill.[vi] It was a challenging time both socially and financially for the family trying to fit into American culture and to make a living during The Great Depression.

The family's Azorean customs of gardening, keeping chickens and pigs did not further the development of neighborly relations on Wakefield Hill. While kitchen gardens were common at that time, the crowing of roosters at the crack of dawn and the slopping of pigs were not, among the Rays' Irish and English abutters. In fact, it was George's household chore to go to each neighbor's door regularly to ask for wet garbage for slop to feed the pigs. As such, he was known in the neighborhood as "the swill boy" landing him in frequent fist fights with the other local boys. George recounted many stories about altercations over ethnic slurs hurled between groups of boys walking home from school and the resulting black eyes. There was no doubt in his mind that the Portuguese were at the bottom of the totem pole in the pecking order of West Warwick society.

The Great Depression presented its own challenges for the family during George's young years. As he wrote himself,

"Then came the lean years, when many of our neighbors began to feel the financial squeeze of the Depression. Many family heads were unemployed and Dad, to put it nicely, was in between jobs. So during the winter months, he worked cutting ice for PePe Laroche (a French Canadian neighbor with an ice house) for fifteen cents per hour. But Dad wasn't one to linger. Through his musical connections, he sought and found employment with the Compton Velvet and Corduroy Company."

Because his father, Frank, was intelligent and spoke English well due to his American education, he rose to the position of foreman at that company in Crompton. Even when work was lean, he was able to bring in extra money by charging for haircuts at home, selling eggs from his own chicken coop, and giving trombone lessons in the front parlor. The children were expected to help as well by "pulling lace" in the evenings at home (more about this in Section Four: The Lace Trade).

There was no doubt that Frank Ray was committed to fully becoming an American and embracing all that this land of opportunity had to offer. In fact, English was the language of the home with Portuguese only spoken between Frank and his wife, Mary, whose own command of English was rudimentary. George states,

"Considering that he had only three years of formal education, my dad was motivated

by a dream to be a good father and citizen in his newly adopted country. His proudest day was becoming a naturalized American citizen at the age of forty-five. He took special delight in playing patriotic songs on his trombone with all his children sitting around singing along with him.

"The following manifests in spirit the love of country my dad held for this his adopted land, and that he wished to instill in his children, the need to respect the symbol of freedom in the American flag:

> *Washington and Jackson, dear old Lincoln, Grant and Lee,*
> *Are the men who made us what we are, on the land and on the sea.*
> *Makes no difference where you wander, makes no difference where you roam,*
> *You don't have to stop to ponder, for a place to call your home.*
> *When they ask you where you're born, lad,*
> *Speak right up, be proud to say:*
> *That your home's the land of Uncle Sam, in the good old U.S.A."*

This was one of the tunes from Frank's musical repertoire that he played and sang with his children and grandchildren, which in fact, some of us recall by heart even to this day.

(1) Some members of the Ray family: (L-R) Frankie, Tommy, Mary, George behind Evelyn c. 1935 on Wakefield Street. (2) Mary and Frank Ray in the early 1940s.

STORIES FROM YOUTH

In spite of the many hardships encountered, George described his childhood as a happy one in a warm and loving home where they didn't have everything they wanted but certainly had everything they needed. He wrote many poems and stories about those early days of his youth focusing on moments during a simpler time when values and expected behavior seemed so much clearer. He often said that "nostalgia is a congenial filter" where only the happiest recollections are allowed to the surface of consciousness. They are best described in his own words.

IF AT FIRST YOU DON'T SUCCEED

"In recording my formative years, age six seems best to recall the depths of my well of memories. I have mentioned in verse, vignettes topical to that timeframe and of periods relating to boyhood days.

"At age fourteen, following my experience of the horrific hurricane of 1938, the ensuing years were void of any ambitious attitude due to the Depression. Leaving school at age sixteen, I sought employment to contribute to our family income. What follows is a laundry list of various jobs, none conducive to a realistic future: worked in a coal yard bagging coal for twenty-five cents per hour, worked a third shift filling batteries in a textile plant, accepted employment in a rubber plant (lasting one day). With the outbreak of war, I worked in a textile finishing plant furnishing cloth for the military, seven days a week, midnight to eight a.m.

"My last job before entering the military was at the Crompton Velvet and Corduroy Company, working by my father's side. He was then a supervisor and a joy to be with, which translated into a happy point in that time of my life. He was both to me a father figure and a friend, one who would never speak in profane language nor hear of any in my presence.

"My first experience of testing the mettle of manhood came when I was challenged to drink a full stein of beer with a whole raw egg nestled in the bottom of it. I contemplated the beer with that one-eyed monster leering back at me waiting for consumption. With

my father cheering me on, I closed my eyes and with an open mouth the monster drifted back into the abyss. I was then accepted into the camp of adulthood which echoed with resonance throughout the bar—the bar of manhood, that is.

"I was never encouraged to drink or smoke to prove my masculinity. Dad would say, well before the U.S. Army coined the tagline, 'Whatever your niche in life, be all that you can be.'"

Some of George's most endearing stories of growing up in the house on Wakefield Street center around the mischief that he and his brother, Alfred, who was older by two years, frequently got into. Through these stories and poems, Dad reveals some of the most lighthearted and humorous moments of his early life.

TOO YOUNG TO DRIVE

On an early Saturday morning,
Visitors at my house arrived.
A touring car parked at the curb,
When Alfred pretended to drive.
He sat behind the steering wheel,
A big shot he appeared to be.
He invited me to sit beside,
In the front seat too low for me.

He made funny motor noises,
And played until he was bored.
Placing me behind the wheel,
Said he would play no more.
While jumping out of the car,
He released the parking brake.
The car began to roll backward,
With my life survival at stake.

Rolling backward, I tightly held the wheel,
And saw the ground passing by.
I didn't know what I should do.
Scared to death, I began to cry.
With Alfred nowhere in sight,
I thought for sure I would die.
The car rolled back 100 feet,
And jumped the neighbor's curb.
It made such a crashing sound,
The noise the owner heard.

It came to rest in a vacant lot,
I, still behind the wheel.
My heart was pounding so,
I had no sense of feel.
Now where would you guess,
Was Alfred's whereabouts?
When I get my hands on him,
I'll punch the dirty lout!

No damage to the touring car,
And the neighbor's curb survived.
My Dad and visitor came a'running,
With a look of some surprise.
To see a six year old behind the wheel,
Unlicensed, too young to drive.
And where would you find Alfred,
For his life was in dread?
Found later in the bedroom,
Hiding safely beneath the bed.

P.S. Such was the beginning of my driving experience.
– Joseph "George" Ray, November, 1994

Josephine, née *Jorgina*, was the high-spirited younger sister of George's mother, *Maria dos Anjos de Faria* / Mary Ferris. She was one of the three sisters who immigrated to the United States from *Rabo de Peixe* with their parents in 1905-1906. There were many summer evenings while visiting Aunt Josephine when we were entertained by her lively stories of her nephews' antics while looking after them. "*Coriscos! Coriscos!*" she said she would yell running after them using the common Portuguese expletive for "rascal" (also the term for a person native of São Miguel).[vii] She had us all in stitches. Consequently, Dad penned the following keeping her spirit and memory alive.

THE PERILS OF AUNT JOSEPHINE

MaMa was hospitalized in the thirties,
For major surgery for discomforts unknown,
Her stay would be for some duration,
And be away for a while from home.
Frankie was a lad of sixteen or so,
Followed by Alfred and me.
Tommy was about five at the time,
Evelyn, the youngest, at three.

My father and Frankie were off at work,
And could not leave us kids alone.
A good paying job Dad could not shirk,
Yet still needed to tend hearth and home.
Dad was concerned for our welfare,
And was in need of someone to care,
That's when Aunt Josephine was summoned,
Of this heavy burden to share.

Aunt Josephine was Mom's young sister,
Who was energetic and always on the go.
And for brevity's sake in my writings,
I'll shorten her name to Aunt Jo.
She was known by many in our village,
As a spitfire of Latin renown.
Messing with her was a big mistake,
If you planned to stay around.

I recall a time she cooked dinner,
Of a chicken my father had plucked.
The fowl was placed in the oven,
With all the condiments and stuff.
But as the bird began to cook,
No one could muster the nerve,
To tell Aunt Jo that the foul odor,
Was from the intestines still in the bird.

Now the day had come for laundering,
Hanging bedsheets and underwear a sight.
She had toiled for hours a'washing,
To get the laundry so bright.
As a boy I harbored thoughts,
To be off gathering nuts.
So helping Aunt Jo to take in the wash,
Was a job I cared for not much.

Now Aunt Jo called for my help,
To gather the laundry and such.
While racing through my mind,
Was to be off a'gathering nuts.
Handing me the clean sheets to hold,

I dropped them and took flight up the road.
In a foot race had she ever caught me,
This story might have never been told.

Well, I managed to outrun her slippered feet,
While off to the meadow I did go.
To pick a bag of wild nuts as a gift,
To appease an angry Aunt Jo.
Now as I approached the house, ill at ease,
She seemed calm, yet still I dread.
She, taking the bag of nuts with a smile,
Promptly whopped me over the head.

I have a paragraph in mind about Alfred,
When Aunt Jo, with nothing to do, was bored.
Alfred suggested there were stockings to mend,
And could be found in the dresser drawer.
With needle and thread in hand, she began,
Sewing like mad, endless it seemed.
What MaMa had saved for braiding rugs,
Unbeknownst to Aunt Josephine.

At last, Mama recovered from surgery,
And returned home discomfort free.
But stories were told of the brats,
In the name of Alfred and me.
Now MaMa and Aunt Jo have passed on,
Into the heavens and beyond.
But now I wax nostalgic remembering,
Chicken dinners, mended stockings,
And white sheets laying soiled on the ground.

– *Joseph "George" Ray, November, 1993*

RUB-A-DUB-DUB IN A LAUNDRY TUB

As you peruse a real estate section,
With regularity one would read,
Of a comfortable house with bath,
In mint condition to see.
It's an accepted standard occurrence,
As common as can be,
To live in a house with indoor plumbing,
With appliances and amenities.

The reason for this prologue follows,
Of a story that begs to be told,
How on a Saturday night at bath time,
A washtub was placed by the stove.
Alfred, my brother, was older you see,
In pecking order demanded to wash before me.
He'd accuse me of wetting,
While in the tub standing,
As water ran down off my wee.

Oh, how he cried he was cleaner than I,
That in washing, I dirtied the water with crud.
The concession to me, if I went out to pee,
He would allow me first in the tub.
Now, Alfred, was a con man and sharp for a kid,
And to no one would give any quarter,
So while I was gone, he would hurry and wash,
Before I could return to the water.

But the moral of the story is,
How MaMa would smile besting Alfred,
At the game she would play,
To get him to stay
In the tub,
For his Saturday scrub.

– *Joseph "George Ray, November, 1993*

HAWKING OUR WARES

Recalling a period in time,
When I was young and brash,
Necessity dictated a need,
Because money at that time was scarce.

The garden I mention,
Was a walking distance from home,
Where sweet corn and potatoes, and other produce were grown.
Cultivating and weeding, not a labor of love,
Brought a productive harvest of more
Than sixty bushels of potatoes,
In excess of our need,
With limited space in the cellar to store.

An agreement was struck,
By PaPa, Alfred, and me,
To sell the excess of our harvest
Of strawberries, corn, potatoes, and peas.
Full of hope and adventure,
A new era was born, With a wagon heaped in vegetables,

Hawking strawberries, peas, potatoes, and corn.
The agreement struck by we three,
Was to sell the produce for a nominal fee,
Fifteen cents for sweet corn, strawberries, and peas,
Ten cents for PaPa and a nickel for Alfred and me.
A little problem arose between Alfred and me,
Who'd do the hawking and selling, don't you see?
Alfred excused himself as he stuttered in speech,
So the hawking and selling were left up to me.

As we proceeded selling our wares,
I would soon be in shock,
After making our first sale,
With money in our sock,
I'll handle the money,
Said Alfred to me,
You do the selling,
And I'll be the secretary.

Such was the beginning,
Of our entrepreneurship,
A lesson learned early,
In my life to be sure.
Accepting the role as seller delegated to me,
Alfred handling the money as secretary.
We went on our way peddling our wares,
Hawking sweet corn, potatoes, strawberries
And garden peas, fresh as the air.

P.S. However, I love my brother Alfred dearly. Brother, Georgie

– Joseph "George" Ray, December 1994

TOMATO PICKING TIME

To appreciate the harvest,
You must first toil in the fields,
A lesson taught at an early age,
To work and experience the feel.

It was a summer in the thirties,
When my dad struck a deal,
To arrange that Alfred and I,
Would work in a tomato field.

To work for Mr. Simas,
It was so agreed,
Would be a lesson to us both,
Of life's responsibility.

So one early morn, Alfred and I,
With lunches packed, and full of pride,
Traveled to Mr. Simas' farm,
By car, a seven mile ride.

Orders were given,
On how to pick and choose,
Tomato boxes stacked dozens high,
On a truck bed with no time to lose.

As soon as a truck bed was loaded,
Alfred would drive it away,
Returning for another load,
Picking more tomatoes I would stay.

Something here is wrong,
I then began to ponder.
Alfred was having a great time back and forth,
That's when I began to wonder.

So when Alfred returned for a refill,
I was seated in the shade,
If you don't help with the picking,
It's here that I will stay.

We managed to complete a working day,
Knowing Mr. Simas was not pleased,
Alfred returned the next day,
And I remained home at ease.

(You can fool George some of the time,
But you can't fool George all of the time.)

– Joseph "George" Ray, August, 1995

Partners in crime George (L) and brother Alfred (R) during their last meeting at Alfred's home in West Warwick, Labor Day Weekend, 2011.

THROW THE BALL OVER

It was a summer in the thirties,
Of boyhood days recalled,
Kids would gather in a vacant lot,
To play a game of ball.
We were a rag-tag bunch of the neighborhood,
With parents unemployed.
Some wore sneakers, some wore shoes,
And some wore none at all.

It was the best of times and the worst of times,
When honesty abound,
And due to the Depression,
There were very few jobs around.
But we made do with what we had,
And were happy and content.
Some had more than others,
While some couldn't pay the rent.

So out of need we managed to make,
The tools of America's game.
The bat was a 2 x 4, or a tree limb cut,
It was all the same.
A golf ball wrapped with cotton and string,
And a penny of friction tape.
We'd knock that old ball around,
Until it was out of shape.

The sides were picked, it made no mind,
Who was best as batter.
Winning was not important to us,
Playing was all that mattered.
Six by six, we'd make up sides,
Three short of what is due.
If you owned a glove, you'd share it,
Whether it was old or new.

Now the field we played in,
Was called the Doucette lot.
It was central to the neighborhood,
Yet, some distance from the park.
The field was small by standard,
With little space to roam.
Where Mr. Doucette and bride-to-be,
Had planned to build a home.

Mr. Doucette was a plumber,
In construction, a man of talent, it was said,
But to his surprise when the cellar was dug,
The diggers struck a ledge.
The story around when construction stopped,
And why he never built his home,
Some say he was low on cash,
And couldn't secure a loan.

Needless to say, no house was built,
And tales told untrue,
The bride-to-be became quite ill,
And died of the dreaded flu.
What happened is a mystery,

As depression took its toll.
Now three score years have passed,
And we kids have grown old.

And if by chance when time permits,
I pass this hallowed ground,
I'll revel in my reverie,
Of all those familiar sounds.
We boys of yesteryear, aged and gray,
With grandchildren of men to be,
To see them play the game we played,
And relive fond memories.

Post Script:
On the vacant lot once echoed in play,
Stands a house this present day,
The vacant lot is a lot no more,
Replaced by memories, I've placed in store.

The following article on the next page was published in the *Pawtuxet Valley Daily Times* along with the photo that inspired the above poem, "Throw the Ball Over" by Joseph George Ray. The group of boys pictured were some of the neighborhood kids who played ball in the Doucette lot. The story goes that the Rays' neighbor, Mrs. LaRoche, gathered the boys together with her camera, instructing them to run home and to return wearing a good white shirt for a photo.

Tuesday, October 15, 1996 • **11**

ors

Front row, from left, Robert LaRoche, Henry Quinn, Johnny Costa, Gilbert and Russell Rego. Second row, Aris and Herman Rego, Willy and Joe Costa, Jimmy LaFerriere, and Louis Furtado who later became Joseph George Ray's brother-in-law. Back row, Sydney Rego and Louis Furtado. The photo was taken by Mrs. LaRoche.

Memories of boyhood days long gone by

Had another fine chat the other afternoon with Joseph George Ray of Greene Street in West Warwick and it was about the boyhood days and the memories of long ago in the Clyde, Phenix and Lippitt areas of West Warwick.

He was quick to say, "Days may come and days may go, but still the hands of memory weave photos that capture time held still.

And he added, "The photo that I am passing along to you has much to do with boyhood days and memories of long ago. Those were the days of innocence, a period of time of respect for our parents and elders and a high regard for the law.

"Though we have witnessed a decline of moral values, we continue to persevere. But still our minds harken back to the days of old, when social values were held in high virtue.

"The photo dates back to 1934 when we could gather centrally in

Amby Smith

the neighborhood to play a game of ball. There were three areas of play to chose from, The Ledge, Doucette's Lot and a long stretch of land suitable for football along Smith Street that was owned by Maisie Quinn.

"She was a gracious lady who allowed us access in this field of play. So too, were 'Pepe' LaRoche of the Ledge and Mr. Doucette, who allowed us to play in a small quadrant of space located off Codfish Hill in the Lippitt section of the town of West Warwick.

"These were venues where friendships were molded into lasting memories. The Ledge was a playground for all seasons with golf and baseball in the summer, and ice skating in the winter that were enjoyed by adults and children alike.

"The frolic play and sounds of laughter poets say, 'Is a symphony in prayer.'"

And in conclusion, Joe went on to say, "These little areas of space afforded us time well spent to grow in character, both in spirit and spirituality."

The young men that Joseph George Ray tells about back in 1934 are: Robert LaRoche, Henry Quinn, Johnny Costa, Gilbert and Russell Rego, Aris and Herman Rego, Willy and Joe Costa, Jimmy LaFerriere, Louis Furtado, Sydney Rego and Norman Afflick.

Deceased are Robert LaRoche, Aris and Sydney Rego, and Louis Furtado. Absent from the group when the photo was taken were Alfred and George Ray.

The following piece refers to the annual *Festa do Espírito Santo*, commonly known as the Holy Ghost Feast, which is still held each year during Labor Day weekend by the Portuguese Holy Ghost Society in the Lippitt section of West Warwick. It is a traditional Azorean celebration, replicated in many parts of the United States where Azorean immigrants have settled.[viii] It is commonly thought that it commemorates the generosity of the 14th century Queen Isabella of Portugal who donated bread to the poor and crowned a small poor boy and girl during the celebration.

MY BUFFALO NICKEL AND THE MAN IN THE HAT

Labor Day signals the ending of summer,
With the scent of fall in the air,
When children make ready to return to school,
And longing to visit the fair.
A coloration of leaves appears in the trees,
Dressed in their autumnal wear,
And the honking of geese appears from the north,
With daylight and dark equal in share.

Happily, I recall visions in mind,
Of parades and carnival times,
When the annual celebration called the Festa,
Brings the distribution of bread, meat, and wine.
It is also a time, with my buffalo nickel in hand,
To rush to the grand celebration.
How will I get there? Forlorn and despaired,
Longing to be among friends and relations.

MaMa would say, the order of the day,
With gypsies around, never to roam,
As I sit on the porch steps to ponder,
I dare not to venture from home.
I can hear the bands in the distance play,
Music familiar to me.
You see, my dad gave lessons on the slide trombone,
On Sundays for a nominal fee.

Now the magical time had arrived,
With my buffalo nickel in hand,
It's off to the grand celebration,
To see Daddy play in the band.
Tommy, my brother, a baby then,
Was fast asleep in the carriage,
It was a brown woven wicker, with wire wheels,
Purchased soon after marriage.

Where to spend my buffalo nickel,
As I watched the merry-go-round,
I'll ride that white horse like the cowboys do,
When they gallop into town.
As I turned around on the carnival ground,
I could see the spinning of a wheel,
A man was calling me to come to the stand,
And said he would make me a deal.

"How much do you have to wager?" he said.
"A win will get you a prize!"
The man wore a funny red hat on his head,
And a twinkle in both of his eyes.
My head was below the top of the stand,

So small I could hardly see.
And through the brilliance of light,
A voice whispered, "Play number three!"

To this day, I know not what happened,
With the spinning of that mirrored wheel.
Only that the man in the funny red hat,
Promised he would make me a deal.
Now in my wildest dreams what was to be,
Would fulfil my boyhood fancy,
"Look here folks what this little boy has won!
Twelve one-pound boxes of candy!"

To this day I know the number I played,
Never appeared on that wheel,
And the man with the funny red hat,
Had a reason for rigging the deal.
Could it be in the past when he was a lad,
A favor to him someone did?
And what better time with a favor past due,
To pass it on to the kid?

Now twelve pounds of candy to carry is heavy,
For a little kid of my size,
Carry a few boxes at a time,
Said the man in the hat, would be wise.
Now as I reminisce that memorable day,
With boxes of candy and carriage in tow,
I wonder now that I'm aged and gray,
What became of the man in the funny red hat,
Who brought joy to a little boy on carnival day.

– Joseph "George" Ray, November, 1993

SNOW COVERED FAIRWAY GREEN

Imagine for a moment if you will,
Sledding down a frozen hill,
Traveling a half mile in distance,
With little or no resistance.
It's a phenomenal occurrence to happen,
Maybe twice in a lifetime to wait,
To have snow with a frozen surface,
Hard enough to support human weight.
It was on this winter occasion,
With a very large sled in tow.
Where the brothers Ray sought adventure,
To slide on this frozen snow.

It was with this sturdy large "flyer,"
That brothers Frankie, Alfred, and me,
Selected the West Warwick Golf Course,
To sled down fairways two and three.
It was a distance of four hundred yards or more,
In the parlance of golf, a par four,
On a very steep slope on an incline,
With a half mile to soar.

As I said, this was a very large sled,
To accommodate all of us three,
Frankie, as the steerer, laid flat,
Straddled-legged by Alfred and me.
I was the "pusher" of motion to get,
To make ready for our descent.
Having no idea of the thrill that await us,
In anticipation of the coming event.

As we started our downhill slide,
Not appraised of this dangerous ride,
Attaining a speed with none to compare,
It was a challenge we jointly shared.
As the cutting wind froze tears to our cheeks,
And our noses and faces stinging red,
A cloud of powdered snow followed our sled,
And in our path, a frozen pond just ahead.

As it turned out the pond was no threat,
As we crossed it incident-free,
With the momentum up another incline,
Stopping on putting green three.
But that ride down the hill,
Was more than just a ride.
You see, it etched a lasting memory,
On the Ray brothers three.

Now, as I walk these fairways green,
I foolishly wonder what it would be,
To sled down those frozen hills again,
With Frankie laid flat and steering,
Straddle-legged by Alfred and me.

Now as a post-script, I make entry this addition,
Of an old cliché worth mention,
That events in life cycle repeat.
Some years later, when Marie was near ten,
That daring sleigh ride was realized again.
Maybe someday, if life's cycle holds true,
The Fraley Family will see, John and Ben take that ride,
On snow covered fairways two and three.

(Sketch by Joseph G. Ray)

Indeed this experience was repeated in the winter of 1960, when on a long "Flexible Flyer" sled, my father and I took that ride down that same fairway hill, not once but three times. He was lying flat on his stomach and I on his back with my arms wrapped around his shoulders. We pushed off and gained an unimaginable speed with the wind rushing by so strong I could hardly breathe as the tears froze to my cheeks. Burying my face in his neck, I can still hear his laughter ringing in my ears as he yelled, "Hang on, Marie! Hang on!"

THAT ELUSIVE SANTA CLAUS

My home off Wakefield Street where I was born,
Runs from Natick to a section of Clyde.
It was a winding country lane,
In length some three miles to ride.
Our home was a little cottage,
From birth through childhood to reside,
Though absent of luxurious comfort,
It was warm and cozy inside.

Holidays to me will ever be,
Recessed deep in my mind,
How Mom and Dad worked so to provide,
Simple joys at Christmastime.
We would hang our stockings behind,
A cast iron stove black as tar,
In hopes to find in the morning,
A Christmas tree topped bright with a star.

As MaMa and PaPa readied for Christmas,
(Affectionately what they were called),
Arctic was the shopping center back then,
There was no such place as a mall.
MaMa did her Christmas shopping,
Quite secretly without a hint to be known.
She would make purchases, these Christmas gifts,
And quietly store them at home.

Now as we prepare for the arrival of Santa,
It was bath time so we may be,
As clean as a shiny new penny,
To dream of toys we would see.
The day was filled with excitement,
Sights and smells of greenery abound.
As window lights twinkled in the neighborhood,
While fresh snow fell covering the ground.

In the dead of winter, after snow had fallen,
And streets were plowed, packed frozen and hard,
You could hear the tire chairs clicking a tune,
As automobiles traveled the road.
In the still of the night, that season,
With snow reflecting the stars and moon so bright,
That clickety clack of chains in rhythm,
Would lull you to sleep at night.

Now we were all tucked away in our beds,
So excited we could hardly sleep.
Someone would say they heard reindeer,
And the trampling of cloven feet.
A thing which seemed an annual request,
That PaPa would promise to me.
When Santa comes down the chimney,
Would you please hold him so that I may see?

We managed somehow to close our eyes,
As tiredness was overtaken by sleep.
All at once our slumber was broken,
By the clatter of noise from the street.
PaPa was shouting that he caught Santa,

Hurry down so he could show,
The remains of a red jacket in hand,
And Santa's boot prints left in the snow!

P.S. I always wondered how PaPa, who was so good in everything he did, could never quite manage to catch Santa?

– Joseph "George" Ray, November, 1994

EVELYN RAY SIMAS

Evelyn was the only daughter and youngest child of Frank and Mary Ray, and without a doubt, the cherished sister of four older brothers. In 1954, she married Ernest Simas, an intelligent and hard-working son of Azorean immigrants, a veteran of the Korean War, who was well known to the family. The man who won Evelyn's hand would certainly have to run the gauntlet of a stern Portuguese father and four equally protective brothers. Evelyn and Ernie were happily married for fifty years, raised two successful children with grandchildren, and built a series of thriving restaurants, primarily because of Evelyn's vision and hard work. She was warm and caring like her mother, and much loved by her extended family of sisters-in-law, nieces and nephews as well as all who knew her.

A LITTLE GIRL DIVINE

Dedicated to sister, Evelyn, who may have felt deprived and not loved by her brothers.

Mom and Dad, often heard to say,
Having brought four boys in a row,
And nary a gift of a girl, prayed
Lord, bring forth to us such a pearl.

It was a prayer to the Lord often heard,
And a blessing to all it would be,
In the future some time when,
A little girl would be christened, Evelyn.

So the message reached the far heavens,
And an order placed in motion,
To deliver a little girl to we earthlings,
An order which caused such commotion.

She was due the first of the year,
Like Frankie, Alfred, and George, for sure,
However, due to an early delivery,
She arrived two months premature.

Landfall was made in November,
Precisely on the thirteenth day near noon,
With a letter under separate cover,
Of the delivery made too soon.

The letter went on explaining,
About a mix-up two years ago,
It concerned the arrival of Tommy,
Who was the only one born in June.

For all we have we are jointly pleased,
With never a thought to forsake,
Born four boys and a little girl divine,
Know God is free of mistakes.

– Brother George, September, 1996

A LETTER TO EVELYN FROM GEORGE

December 10, 1996

Dear Evelyn,

Of the many benefits provided by retirement, I find that reminiscing about past events comes most clearly to me resting in my recliner on some lazy afternoon. I think about how we are genetically bound as a family as brothers and sister. Although we are different in personalities, we share the hopes and aspirations that MaMa and PaPa held for their children.

I was reminded of this when I visited you last Monday, and how graciously you showed me the fruits of your labor in the decorating of the Villa with all the Christmas trappings. That's when my thoughts traveled for a brief moment, thinking how proud MaMa and PaPa would be to see what their little girl had accomplished. I believe (certain that a God exists) that you are the fulfillment of what MaMa and PaPa had hoped and dreamed.

I think back some years ago when I ran for tax assessor and was declared the front runner on the Wednesday after Election Day. I was at work when I received a telephone call from PaPa congratulating me on my victory. Though it was never to be, and short-lived, his was a voice of happiness which still rings in my mind. I know for certain that Frankie, Alfred, and Tommy could share similar experiences, however, I can only speak for myself.

So, Evelyn, thank you for being you. Thank you for the cordial way in which I am greeted when I do pay you a visit, and for making all us brothers proud of you, as proud as our parents are in their heavenly home.

See you soon,

(Signed)
Brother George

MY MOTHER'S DAUGHTER

Since her passing on October 18, 1974, I have had no dreams of my mother. It seems as though my subconscious has sheltered my mind from any spiritual contact where I could experience once again the joy of being near to my mother. Recently one evening, it happened and a most pleasant dream it was. In my dream, my mother appears in an odd and fascinating event in which she refers to my sister but not by name.

I had a dream an evening past,
In heaven I tenderly held my mother's hand.
We walked and talked along a seaside rim,
Marked by footprints on shores of sand.

Gleefully in laughter, of memories shared,
In a euphoric glowing diaphanous light,
On gossamer wings in some defying force,
Cradled closely in gentle flight.

Free of fear in suspended realm,
A journey I'd hope would never end,
And then, seemingly, in wispy evanesce,
A promise of a surrogate she'd send.

"Remember well, your Mother's daughter,
Born in me of dreams you seek,
Regale her with earthly tidings,
In loss of me you need not weep.

When again, in flights of fancy,
Venture forth in dreams you auger,
In requiem of memories past,
Remember well, your Mother's daughter."

– Joseph "George" Ray, October, 1996

Evelyn Ray with her mother, Maria dos Anjos / Mary Ray, 1952 in front of the family home on Wakefield Street.

THE NO NAME HURRICANE

George was only an eighth grader when the Hurricane of '38 hit southern New England on September 21. The experience was still so vivid in his memory that he was able to pen his recollections years later. Because the hurricane took place in 1938 prior to meteorologists naming hurricanes alphabetically with female names, he dubbed the storm, the "No Name Hurricane."

"Fall was late in arriving this third week of September, and foliage appeared to be in no haste to display its usual panoply of colors. With two rain-soaked days, the earth was softened and muddy. The forecast for the next day, Wednesday, was for clearing skies. Nothing seemingly was out of place weatherwise for New England, other than we were enjoying an extended Labor Day retreat. Along with shore dwellers and vacationers, we inlanders were taking advantage of this protracted summer. The marinas were fully occupied by sailing and motor craft of all shapes and manner of forms, although many were making ready for their departure the coming weekend.

"I was an eighth grader and was dismissed as usual at 2:30 p.m. No one was aware of impending weather nor had any knowledge that at that precise time Cape Hatteras and coastal states north of it were in the throes of destruction. As the storm moved north-northeast, it was laying waste to all forms of communication with no chance of alerting those in areas in its path. As communications were being decimated, coastal areas were swept by tidal waves the likes of which seasoned seafarers and coastal dwellers had not witnessed in a lifetime.

"It was a day of infamy in terms of Mother Nature's wrath, which since has been chronicled in many languages, of suffering, the death of hundreds, and property damage in the millions of dollars. It was noted that an anemometer at the Hillsgrove Weather Station[ix] recorded 180 mph winds before it, too, was swept away by stronger gusts.

"As a fourteen year old, this was the day I came of age. Experiencing this force of nature, one comes to the realization that worldly things are of little consequence. The need to survive becomes the primary concern. The sight of trees of one hundred years' maturity being uprooted and falling before me was a nightmare of epic proportion. Roofing shingles were flying through the air like frisbees as I made my way home. It was 3:30 p.m. and the No Name Hurricane of September 21, 1938 was upon us!

"What is this horror that holds us hostage? None of us had ever known winds of this velocity, or even had the word "hurricane" in our vocabulary. The little three bedroom cape, which housed a family of seven, was like a small ship lost at sea, buffeted by winds so great that at times the house was raised several inches off its foundation. The interior pressure between partitions and subfloors was such that it raised carpets and linoleum from the floor. Windows rattled. Debris was everywhere, much of it airborne like missiles in Star Wars. This was the largest hurricane to date in this area measuring three hundred miles across.

"The strength of the storm was unyielding as it continued to pound relentlessly throughout the night. Then, seemingly on command, the wind stopped. Lacking knowledge in meteorology, this cessation gave us a false and short-lived sense of security. We did not know that we were experiencing the calm of the eye of the storm, and that our travails were far from over.

"When the storm first approached, the winds were blowing from west to east carrying ocean spray some twelve miles from shore. It was later learned that the salt spray contaminated grape arbors and fruit trees, and corroded electrical insulation. Once the winds resumed, it was now blowing from west to east with most of the destruction that had fallen to the left were now being thrown to the right. Such was the lesson of this our first experience with a major hurricane.

"My recollection of events that occurred fifty-six years ago is somewhat vague as I struggle to remember, however, what does remain clear in my mind is the uncertainty of how and when this horror would end. The unknown of a second phase of destruction was, to say the least, frightening as we braced ourselves for several more hours of emotional torment and impending destruction. Moreover, of one thing I was keenly aware: there were no professed atheists around that day. It wasn't until early morning when the winds abated and anxieties calmed that blessed sleep finally came to the Ray family of Wakefield Street.

"As we greeted the early morning with trepidation, we were surprised at what little damage was done to our house, save for a number of shingles ripped from the roof. Others were less fortunate where extensive damage was done. Electrical power would not be restored for weeks. Schools were closed and many institutions were slow to recover. The months to follow found many without resources due to the Depression. Noteworthy were the community efforts in full evidence where anyone who could help pitched in.

"We have since experienced many subsequent hurricanes, all with given names, but what made the storm of '38 special is that it heralded the need for accurate information about the behavior of storms and the necessity to communicate warnings in a timely manner. There were no satellites by which to monitor locations and track paths *and wind strengths of impending weather. The Hurricane of September 1938 was an awakening of the need to develop the technology that could develop an early warning system for the many who would be in harm's way."*

Joseph "George" Ray
September 21, 1994

Much of the text of this piece was quoted in the *Kent County Daily Times*, Seniors Column by Amby Smith, Senior Scene Editor, "Memories of the monster they called 'No-Name Hurricane,'" September, 1996.

The Ray family home on 60 Wakefield Street after the hurricane of 1938. The house number was later changed to 95. Note the tree in front of the house stripped bare of all limbs due to the high winds.

THE DEATH OF THE HINDENBURG

The following eye-witness account of Dad's experience as a boy of thirteen of the Hindenburg passing above his junior high school was published in Amby Smith's "Seniors" column on May 2, 1996, fifty-nine years after its occurrence.

"The date was May 6, 1937 and, according to the Perpetual Calendar, the sixth fell on a Thursday. It was a beautiful spring day, and we, at Deering Junior High School, were enjoying recess. If memory serves me correctly, it was near the noon hour.

"Suddenly, there were cries of excitement in the air as a large dirigible appeared seemingly suspended above. It seemed so near that passengers could be seen waving from the ship's passenger decks. The splendor of it was a sight to behold as motors in full view and sound purred in unison.

"The flight path passed over the Royal Mill, in the River Point section of West Warwick, casting a shadow that shaded our entire school yard. The markings of the dirigible were unknown to us until our teacher recognized it as German origin. Swastikas emblazoned on the tail's rudder were symbolic of Hitler's Third Reich as it sailed smoothly out of sight.

"The accounts on the evening news in anticipation of this event reported that "the German zeppelin Hindenburg, with ninety-seven passengers and crew aboard on its twelfth westward voyage across the Atlantic completing a goodwill mission, will be mooring at Lakehurst, New Jersey at 6:00 p.m. EDT."

"The next day at school was charged with concern and excitement as we recounted with disbelief the disaster and death of the dirigible. The Hindenburg, with ninety-seven passengers and crew became a fireball of cataclysmic proportion. Of the ninety-seven aboard, thirty-six lives were lost in the searing wreckage. We later learned through our science teacher that the Hindenburg was inflated with hydrogen, a gaseous element, and although fourteen times lighter than air, was highly flammable.

"Our then Secretary of the Interior, Henry Wallace, knowing of Hitler's warlike predisposition negated the sale of helium gas, which is non-flammable, to Germany. The Roosevelt Administration in its subsequent foreign policy refused to sell any material to Germany that would advance Hitler's warlike aims.

"Hitler went on to create havoc in Europe precipitating a crisis that led to World War II. Conjecture expressed in commentaries suggested that the "goodwill missions" were a ruse to photograph military installations in the United States. It is interesting to surmise whether aerial photographs taken en route might have been destroyed in the dirigible disaster."

THE LEDGE AND PEPE LAROCHE

The following article and sketch appeared in the Letters to the Editor of the *Pawtuxet Valley Times* on January 19, 1995. It was written about the property that abutted the Ray house on Wakefield Street, and its owner, PePe Laroche, where neighbors enjoyed winter and summer activities. The original pencil sketch depicting the Ledge was drawn by Joseph "George" Ray.

Opinion
Letters to the Editor
The Ledge and PePe Laroche

Pawtuxet Valley Times, Thursday, January 19, 1995, p. 5.

Heather in the meadow, rivulets of water seeping through rock crevices converging to form a bubbling stream, the parcel of land, known colloquially as "The Ledge", was a playground for all seasons. The Ledge, once mined for wall stone evidenced by drill holes and surgical partings, left a smooth face of some twenty feet from top to base and some distance across.

Winter's venue turned this site into a frozen, aqueous wonderland forming a citadel of ice increasing in size on the wall surface into a miniature glacier. Water flowing into the basin created a frozen, shallow pond which attracted dozens of children and adult skaters.

PePe Laroche, who owned the Ledge, was a Canadian descent and followed in a tradition of ice cutters. Long before electrical refrigeration, ice was basic for preserving foods. PePe's several large ponds in Blackrock and Fiskeville, when frozen deep, would provide the harvesting of tons of ice stored in a large icehouse which was insulated by hay and sawdust to keep the ice from melting during the summer months.

In the absence of trucks, horse drawn wagons were used to transport cuttings to the icehouse and too, made home and commercial deliveries.

Many mornings I could hear PePe in the barn (which was in earshot of my house) disciplining his horses in his native french. When I asked my Dad, also fluent in French, what PePe was saying, Dad would say that PePe was talking to the animals and was making certain who was boss. On one point we were served notice "Never repeat what you hear in French or any other language."

Summers transformed this bucolic land into a green grazing area for PePe's horses and milk cow. Nevertheless, there were ample space in which to design a crude two hole golf course. With one golf club and ball we conducted our mini tournaments. Occasionally errant shots ricocheting from rock to rock would come to rest near the intended hole. In addition, climbing the ledge facing with reinformed clothes-line rope was an adventure. Clearing a quadrant of the meadow we fashioned a ballfield and between abandoned ledge cuttings, built little camp sites. Also, what I hold dear is the memory of the basin pond as a habitat for peeping toads and frogs. The population would multiply in numbers so great that the crocking and "ribbits" would echo throughout the meadow in a summer symphony. Moreover, last but not least, my greatest reason to recall these memories would be of PePe himself who never refused us access to the Ledge and delegated himself as his brother's keeper. Although, the industry of ice harvesting has faded and rest now in the past, memories of the Ledge, PePe and family linger warmly with me.

Joseph G. Ray
West Warwick

The Ledge is located off Wakefield Street in the Lippitt section of town, remains in the Laroche Family in the name of Pepe's great grandson, Michael.

This poem was published in the Poetry Corner of the Pawtuxet *Valley Daily Times* and caused quite a bit of speculation about the identity of the mystery subject of the love letters.

LOVE LETTERS NEVER SENT

This is a story in verse of a young boy too awkward and shy to pursue the attention of a young girl far too beautiful for him. However, he lived vicariously fantasizing, if...

> Had she read the letters he never sent,
> Of his secret love she would have known,
> When she lived nearby just up the road,
> Love letters he'd written so long ago.
>
> Recalling, as if it were yesterday,
> She greeted him as she walked by,
> With eyes of blue, and friendly smile,
> He was speechless and mesmerized.
>
> His dreams were not to him a waste,
> Planning to meet with her again,
> And hold her hand as often then,
> At an amusement park or a Nickelodeon.
>
> Then one day she moved away,
> She smiled and waved as she drove by,
> Never knowing how he loved her then,
> Had she read the letters he didn't send.

Times of sadness are memories passed,
And in gladness memories last,
Though brief in time memories still,
In life we journey in different paths.

When sadly he read that she passed away,
And recalls with warmth of days gone by,
Her eyes of blue and radiant smile,
When he was a boy awkward and shy.

At a flower shop he chanced to pick,
In remembrance of what might have been,
When asked, "Who might the sender be?"
With a faint smile replied, "A friend."

At a grave site covered by a blanket of snow,
She rests beneath flowers frozen and rent,
And nestled in gardenias of white and blue,
Lie faded love letters never sent.

Recalls he, as a boy, in days of yore,
That she in his flights of fancy adored,
Still wondering now what might have been,
Had she read the letters he was too shy to send.

– Joseph "George" Ray, West Warwick

The following piece appeared in the *Kent County Daily Times* in Letters to the Editor, January 6, 1995. Dad recounted to me what it was like for this rag-tag group of trade shop boys in John Kelly's and Gus Olson's classes. As football coaches, they knew how to handle adolescent boys.

TEACHERS WHO INSPIRED ME

"The teachers who inspired me were Messrs. John Kelly and Gus Olson. Neither held to the philosophical tenet that slow learners were dumb or lazy nor to the adage that "you can't make a silk purse out of a sow's ear." Messrs. Kelly and Olson experienced the hardships of the financial depression of the 20s and 30s so recognized basic deprivations within their student enrollment. Mr. Kelly taught History/Current Events, while Mr. Olson taught English/Literature. In addition, they coached football in tandem: Mr. Kelly as head coach on offense, and Mr. Olson as defensive coordinator.

"I was an introverted sophomore in the (then) Westcott High School and harbored a timidity towards teachers in general. I was less than an average grade student, moving from K to 9 struggling to maintain a C average. However, my inhibitions seem to dissolve upon entering the classes of these gentle giants. And, too, did my attitude change and motivation accelerate by their non-threatening persona. In retrospect, I believe they were gifted with an innate sense, recognizing attention deficit disorder and/or dyslexia before those diagnoses of medical science were known.

"Mr. Kelly encouraged open discussions relating to events past, present and a clairvoyance of what cause and effect might generate future developments. This would instill confidence in us, that we were not dumb or lazy and that it was all a matter of hard work and application. Mr. Olson's principle belief was: "If you speak correctly, you communicate correctly." Assigning a few words a day, we were force-fed repetitiously in spelling and word usage, followed by a week-end test. This would continue exponentially with new word usage added to our ever growing vocabulary. Soon our class, that was previously viewed as marginal, now enjoyed high grade averages. That we were a rowdy, all-boys class who learned to focus our interest and good behavior was a credit to remarkable teaching skills.

"New changes occurred with the passing of time. Some went on to higher learning. For others, their education interrupted by war joined the military in defense of their country, served with honor, and were awarded medals of distinction. Therefore, in some manner or form, a suitable place of honor should be considered as a fitting tribute in a TEACHERS' HALL OF FAME in recognition of service to their community, and to give solace to their families (proud loved ones all)."

A lifelong resident of West Warwick, Class of '42
Joseph G. Ray, West Warwick

A follow-up article appeared in Amby Smith's Seniors Column on February 4, 1997 citing Dad's reflections of John Kelly and Gus Olson as teachers, but also, being a local sports columnist for many years, Amby included a detailed account of their athletic abilities and contributions to high school interscholastic football.

As part of his research, Dad visited Mr. Kelly's widow, Mrs. Doris Kelly. She was so appreciative of Dad's kind words that she gave him a pair of her husband's bookends. After that, she frequently dropped him notes praising and encouraging his writings considering him a friend.

Mr. John Kelly had a long and successful career in the West Warwick School Department. I personally remember him well as the principal of the newly constructed West Warwick Senior High School on Arctic Hill when I attended from 1965 to 1968. I was impressed that he knew and addressed every single student by name: boys were "Mr. _____" and girls were "Miss _____." During school assemblies, he made it clear that it was expected that everyone would become silent and attentive as soon as a speaker approached the podium—and we all did without reminders or prompting. Students were respected and were expected to be respectful in turn.

TO SIR WITH LOVE

In tribute to Francis Gibney, my 9th grade teacher, who laid down for me a foundation of principle behavior, which paid great dividends in the pursuit of learning.

> *How can I thank you,*
> *For memories I hold dear?*
> *The calendar reads time has passed,*
> *Years gone by, yet in memory so near.*
>
> *In reminiscing my classroom days,*
> *I recall classics read clear to ponder,*
> *Those adventures played out in epilogue,*
> *Though long ago still resounding.*
>
> *Our dark hair now silver gray,*
> *And walking gait, slowed just a snip,*
> *But the memories of classroom days,*
> *Have faded not one bit.*
>
> *The classroom now a silent void,*
> *With desktops shrouded in gossamer veil,*
> *And as your resonant voice dances in my mind,*
> *Though long ago, cherish memories to regale.*
>
> – *Joseph "George" Ray, April 7, 1997*

"School days, school days, dear old golden rule days, Reading, and writing and 'rithmetic..."

"While recently rummaging through a collection of old books, I came across a treasure trove of classics. Among them were such hard cover works as "A Tale of Two Cities," "Romeo and Juliet," and "Treasure Island." These are among many of the classics I enjoyed while attending the ninth grade at the then John F. Deering Junior High School.

"We were a collection of thirty-five active, and sometimes unruly, boys, assigned to Mr. Frank Gibney's class. Most of all of us boys, with a few exceptions, were not college bound, due to either a lack of motivation or economic priorities. No doubt a monumental challenge, Mr. Gibney found how to best capture the attention of thirty-five restless boys.

"I believe in retrospect that Mr. Gibney's background had much to do with his plan in reading these riveting classics to us. Mr. Frank Gibney left his beloved country of the Emerald Isle (Drogheda, Ireland) at the age of nine to take up residence with relatives. By accounts related to me by my grandparents, young Frank Gibney, was in the care of an aunt, Mrs. Bridget Gibney Flanagan, who saw to young Frank's needs through his formative years. My grandparents who lived across the street from the Flanagans, always welcomed young Frank into their home recalling that he was a polite and handsome young lad whose face radiated with a broad smile. It would be years later, when I was a young student and he was my teacher, that he recalled with fond memories those Christmas and Easter holidays spent at my grandparents' home. This revelation did not in any way guarantee me a passing grade. It did, however, make me feel at ease and more discerning.

"We ninth graders were given little choice but to behave, because Mr. Gibney was a mountain of a man. In size and demeanor, he was an imposing figure. Moreover, what was first viewed as a threat to us soon evaporated, as we listened attentively to his reading of these interesting classics. We were all so consumed by the rhythm and cadence of his melodious baritone voice that some would begin to nod off. It was at this point when the "pooning" of blackboard chalk took place. How he could simultaneously read and spot nodding heads remained a mystery to us as well as his on target accuracy.

"Clearly, after all was said and done and as I reminisce about the past, I realize his purity of purpose. By reading these classics, he imparted the correct formulation of sentences and an understanding of communication in speech patterns that we, later in years, could emulate. For to imitate in a positive way is said to be paid the highest form of compliment."

Part One: Early Life

Parts of Dad's above text were quoted and cited in Amby Smith's Seniors column of the *Kent County Daily Times* on March 18, 1997, "Frank Gibney: A gifted teacher remembered over the years." Mr. Gibney was still living at the time the article was published and was very touched by the tribute. Handwritten notes from his wife to my father, included in the Addenda at the end of this book, related that he "got a kick out of" the "pooning of chalk" reference. He said that he remembered that class well. He was a teacher for 47 years also serving as Vice-Principal of West Warwick Junior High School. He died at the age of eighty-eight on November 6, 1997 a few months after the article was published.

Part Two:
Military Service

When Dad started to retrace the steps of his military service in the Army during World War II, he spent much time in the library reading about the battles, the marches, and the routes that his company took. He wanted a bird's eye view of the strategies of which he was a part on the ground and in the mud. He wanted to get it right, to frame the correct context because he said, "I want my grandsons to know what we did and what we fought for, but not the gory stuff, just why it was important."

Like many patriotically spirited young men of draft age in the early 1940s, George Ray heeded the call to arms to defend freedom and country once the United States was drawn into World War II after the bombing of Pearl Harbor on December 7, 1941. He followed his older brother, Alfred, who enlisted in the U.S. Army in November of 1942 by enlisting himself in March of 1943. Their eldest brother, Frankie, already married in 1940, in turn followed them by enlisting in September of 1943. Therefore, Frank and Mary Ray had both the honor and the anxiety of three sons serving simultaneously in Europe in the U.S. Army during World War II.

What follows is George's account of his impressions and experiences in his own words:

"It was the middle of December, 1941. Japan had attacked Pearl Harbor and we found ourselves in the throes of war. I was a young man of seventeen and was ambivalently distressed and excited by these events and what the outcome would be.

"That winter evening remains vivid in my mind. It was a clear starlit night with the sliver of a crescent moon slanted on a tilt hanging in the dark sky. (Fable has it that if you can hang a powder horn on its lower tip that it was a sign of a wet winter.) As I rounded the corner approaching our home, the little cottage was silhouetted by long shadows belying its true shape. A white column of smoke danced from the chimney top carrying the delightful scent of barbecued fish.

"Entering the house, Mom was busy and said Dad was in the cellar hinting that a little company would be appreciated. The cellar was in darkness apart from the firelight emitting from an open furnace door. Dad was seated in front of a coal-fire with a handheld wire grate barbecuing sardinhas, a common fish enjoyed among the Portuguese population here and at home in the Azores.

"My Dad was something of an enigma and yet, a very loving father. He was not one to show affection by hugging or touching. You could no more hug a hot coal-fired furnace than hug my father; however, this did not diminish the love he felt for his family. I sensed that he was troubled by the thought of the war and having three sons of eligible age, and a fourth soon to be, was weighing heavily on his mind. I touched his arm and tried to reassure him that we should hope for the best. Looking deep into the furnace fire with tears in his eyes, he said, 'War is hell!'

"Excusing his watery eyes to the furnace smoke, knowing he had much to worry about, I sat silent, mesmerized by the dancing tongues of flame. Again my thoughts drifted to the adage of the tilted quarter moon and of signs portending a wet season foreboding the tears that would be shed for the loss of loved ones. It was a time of blackout shades obliterating advent lights in windows while dread held hopes and aspirations in abeyance. Those were among the joyless interruptions which nagged at our peace of mind at Christmas that year and for some time to come.

"At the age of sixteen, when my muscles were years ahead of my brains, earning money was then paramount to establishing one's success in life - or so

I thought. Education seemed a waste of time to me and the very thought of pursuing academic achievement bored me. I was encouraged by my teachers to stay in school, but sadly, I realized the value of an education too late to redirect my psyche to higher learning.

"I left school after my sixteenth birthday and took a job in a coal yard bagging coal for fifteen cents an hour. My first pay was $5.95 all tucked neatly in a little brown envelope. Such was the beginning of my odyssey in life. I soon found myself in a number of jobs, the second no better than the many to follow. As we were at war with Japan by virtue of the attack on Pearl Harbor, I found many job opportunities at wage levels never imagined as men were called away to serve in the military. So, the rewards of earned income gave me a false sense of well-being which carried me through the following months."

YOU'RE IN THE ARMY NOW

"The war in the South Pacific drew the United States into the European conflict against Germany and Italy. Soon the urge to be a part of this patriotic wave moved me to join the military. This announcement evoked considerable displeasure from my parents who felt it best that I wait to be called by the draft board. I thought otherwise and set a date to enter what I hoped would be the U.S. Navy. It seemed, however, that I waited too long beyond my eighteenth birthday and soon learned that all Navy enlistments were at full quota. When quotas opened again, I was now of draft age and my only recourse was to volunteer to be drafted into the Navy. This I did and passed the physical but then again, I was told that the Navy was at full strength and that I should return home and wait to be called with the proviso that should the Army call me in the interim, then I would be the property of the Army.

"At this point in time, I had had my fill of testing, so reluctantly, I opted for the U.S. Army. I reported for induction on March 3, 1943, was processed at Fort Devens, Massachusetts, and transported by troop train to Fort Shelby, Mississippi where I received seventeen weeks of basic training in the 623rd Light Equipment

Engineering Company. It was not as glamorous as the title may indicate, but equal to the Navy Seabees, or so they said. This at least gave me hope of an occupation of worth.

"As an afterthought, I do believe that had I graduated from high school, chances are that I may have been accepted into the Navy. So much said for the lack of an education.[x]

BASIC TRAINING

"I weighed 147 pounds when I entered the service and lost 20 pounds of my meager bulk before basic training ended. Although very lean, I felt stronger then than at any time in my life.[xi] *I was given an aptitude test and found that I had a degree of talent in the field of automotives so was assigned as a mechanic to the motor pool. With the passing of time, I scored well enough to earn a promotion to the rank of Private First Class (PFC). Not great, but a start, nonetheless.*

"Physical requirements were very demanding to the point of exhaustion. Daily marching came as second nature to us. Long distance marches of 24 miles with a field pack and rifle in a time span of seven hours tested the hardiest among us. The worst test yet to come was the dreaded infiltration course. It was the length of a football field, strung with barbed wire 36 inches above the ground with open craters charged with explosives and machine guns firing live ammunition above our heads. We had to crawl the full distance on our stomachs with our rifle cradled in our arms. Reaching the end was, to say the least, very humbling.

"My grandmother Ray, Antónia dos Santos Correia, passed away at the time I reached the staging area. Through the Red Cross, I was able to arrange an emergency pass home. Spending those few days at home sleeping in my own bed was a heavenly experience that I had taken for granted. The thought of returning to camp struggled within me. It was not long after returning to camp that we were placed on alert. Soon we were packed and trucked to the docks where we boarded our ship and made ready to sail to destinations unknown.

CROSSING THE ATLANTIC

"Our ship was called the *Santa Barbara*, a converted 26,000-ton oil tanker that accommodated some 500 troops plus cargo in the center hold of the ship. We were never told of the nature of the ship's cargo. I was mostly preoccupied with where we were headed and how I would adjust to the ship's movement, i.e. seasickness. We were fed and told to retire for the night. Tired from the day's activities, sleep came quickly.

"At early morning, we were awakened by the ship's rocking and soon discovered we were on our way. Climbing steel stairways, I made my way topside and, to my surprise, saw ocean waves twenty to thirty feet high. We were now in the Atlantic and well on our way. It remains long in my memory, a most amazing sight, a convoy of one hundred and fifty ships of all descriptions as far as the eye could see. You could actually see the curvature of the earth as ships in the far distance began to appear one by one over the horizon. Our ship, the *Santa Barbara*, was positioned in the middle of the convoy and, as we later learned, was the flagship that commanded this vast armada. The waves were larger now than before as nearby ships would disappear and reappear like toys in this vast watery expanse.

"I was curious as were others, about our compass heading believing that we would be sailing due east toward England. To our surprise, the ships were headed south. It was a game we played in amateurish fashion by counting sailing days and charting the morning sun. Interested by our curiosity, the ship's officer told us that the reason for taking a circuitous route was to avoid German submarines in the area. Heading south and then taking the shoreline route enabled us to stay under the umbrella cover of aircraft protection that was in flying radius of our convoy.

"We arrived in England in early January of 1944 in the seaport of Liverpool, safe and grateful that we had arrived intact. I was, however, overcome by a case of homesickness, an experience for which I was not prepared. The realization of being so far from home was suddenly a startling revelation. Also surprising to me was that the many ships of our convoy seemed to have vanished to parts unknown.

"After we boarded troop trains and were underway, I was amazed at the extent of property damage along our route of travel. German aerial assaults had mercilessly pounded a town called Coventry, of interest to me because our neighboring town at home bears the same name. After many hours of travel, we were lodged in private houses rented by the military called "billets." As many as twelve men shared a unit. My billet was called the "Victory Snack Bar," a former variety store. The reason for dispersing the men was a safety measure against a total wipeout in the event of a direct hit. The Allies controlled the air during daylight hours between 6 a.m. and 11 p.m. Any aircraft flying at night was considered enemy aircraft. You could set your clock by 'Bed Check Gerry' because at 11 p.m., the Germans would unleash their aerial assault. As we made our way to the shelters, I could hear the stoic voices of the local gentry saying, 'Welcome to England, Yanks!' The English citizenry were accustomed to these nighttime raids and moved about with stoic behavior. With blankets and in nightwear, they readied themselves for an evening of aerial onslaught. Showing false bravado that was surely ill-disguised, we were clearly shaken by this experience.

ODE TO SOLDIER JOHNNY STROHM

"My 'buddy,' Johnny Strohm, and I were both billeted at the Victory Snack Bar in Wokingham. Johnny was the son of a New York City Irish police officer and followed in his father's Christian tradition of being pure of heart and mind.

"We were hard at work, training and preparing for the invasion of France and the landing on its beachhead, what was later known as Normandy. Johnny, as mentioned, was a fine Christian man and loved to speak in verse, and as a consequence, recited many rhymes to me. One that still runs through my mind was about the boarding house of Mrs. McGill. So I offer his version of the ditty in memory of a dear friend, living or dead, as I do not know of his whereabouts.

'Mrs. McGill ran a boarding house, Not too far from a company mill, Where she took in boarders, and Without hesitation, presented their rooming bill. It *was said she was a bit frugal, Of meals prepared and fed. Now for your pleasure, I present to you, The following menu that read:*

On Monday, we were served bread and gravy, On Tuesday, it was gravy and bread, Wednesday and Thursday, was gravy and toast, That's nothing but gravy and bread. So on Friday we spoke to the landlady, Won't you please give us something different instead? So for Saturday's dinner by way of a chance, We had gravy without any bread!'

God love you, Johnny,
Joseph George Ray, AKA "Blackie"
November, 1993

George "Blackie" Ray (L) and his buddy, Johnny Strohm (R), in Lambach, Austria in April of 1945 just before the end of the war. Dad's army buddies called him "Blackie" because of the coal black color of his hair. Dad never saw Johnny again after the war, but our research later discovered that he died on October 11, 1997 in Ocala, Florida.

HURRY UP AND WAIT

"The town of Wokingham in Berkshire was a quaint and interesting place with narrow cobblestone roadways, that were difficult to negotiate with our large Army trucks. While our quarters were scattered around town, Central Headquarters was within walking distance of every billet as well as the medical unit where we took meals. By living among the citizenry, it took little time to adjust as we blended into their way of life. There were cinemas, pubs, and even an IGA store nearby that we sometimes frequented making purchases of whatever was not rationed. One little problem that arose which drew displeasure from our English friends was our aggressive nature. Having an abundance of little luxuries, such as candy, cigarettes, and money, caused resentment among the English and Canadian soldiers which surfaced in the form of fistfights in the pubs. Of course, I was rarely involved.

"Six months passed quickly, and the rumors of an impending invasion grew to reality. True to speculation, on the morning of June 6, 1944, the skies were darkened with thousands of aircraft heading east. With cheers rising to the rooftops, it was D-Day and the invasion was on!

"Our equipment had already been prepared with water-proofing compound applied to the engine ignition systems to enable the vehicles to tread in depths of four to five feet. It was not until much later that the order came to move out. Packed, ready, and traveling under sealed orders, our company positioned itself in the southeastern corner of England in the seaport of Southampton.

"On June 8, equipment was loaded aboard LCT crafts.[xii] The memory of that evening that lingers in my mind was that it rained heavily throughout that night. Moving about in ankle deep mud gave me the feeling of being like cattle in a stockyard as it was a most uncomfortable enclosed atmosphere. It was an unexpected wait because most of the day was spent doing what is too often done in the military, hurry up and wait. Finally, we headed out across the English Channel.

"What was expected to be a short crossing, lasted throughout the night.[xiii] The journals of history now tell us the reason for the delay was due to a ren-

dezvous of ships prior to the crossing. The crossing was in darkness although it was light enough to see large balloons anchored to positioned ships to ward off low flying enemy aircraft. At early morning, I could see on the horizon a distant Normandy Beach. One note of interest, my mother had sent me a bag of uncooked beans which the LCT cook obligingly prepared for me. It remains with me after many years, a little act of kindness that dwells still in my memory. It was shared by all creating a kindred spirit among us.

INTO THE BREACH

"*As the sun began to rise in the east, we were in position for our landing. The ramp door opened like the jaws of a whale. Truck engines started up and down the ramp I went into some five feet of water praying the truck engine would behave properly. We continued to tread water for several hundred yards as the Beach Master directed us into position. Thankfully, we made it to the hilltop celebrating in silent prayer, however, the celebration was a bit premature. The engines began to falter. Without hesitation I raised the hood and began removing the molten waterproofing compound from the spark plugs which had overheated and were failing. To my delight, the engine responded well. The word was passed down the line and, as if on cue, a choreography of truck hoods popping up in succession could be seen. As the vehicle engines responded, the unit began moving again. I cannot say it with any certainty, but perhaps it was not by coincidence that I was awarded my corporal stripes a short time later.*

"*The news via the grapevine reported that the first invasion force had penetrated some ten miles inland which gave cause for celebration, but the good news was short-lived as I began to face the fear of the unknown. For the first time, I could hear the sounds and see the clouds of explosions in the not too distant front line. Strange as it may seem, with all this chaos of bombing going on around me, I had not yet seen the enemy. As I recall, my mind and my body were running on instinct. I knew not where I was headed, just that I continued driving through this labyrinth of confusion. I have* no recall in detail of how I made my way from the hilltop to our campsite in a sector called Trevieres.[xiv] I can remember with some clarity, the beginning of this odyssey, but what else happened in between I cannot recall now fifty years later. Nevertheless, of greater importance, I survived landing in Normandy at Omaha Beach.

"We had moved to several overnight bivouac areas before frontal forces were halted. The Germans were putting up strong resistance in their retreat. One factor working against us was that our tanks were suffering great losses due to hedgerows. For centuries, Norman farmers fenced their fields with solid ramparts of earth, often four feet high, surmounted by hedges whose tangled roots bind each row into a natural fortification. When our tanks tried to ride over the tops of these hedgerows, it would expose the vulnerable underbelly of the tank to enemy bazookas. The problem was solved when an Army Sergeant named Culin, came up with the idea of mounting steel tusks on the front of each heavy tank allowing them to tear through the hedgerows.[xv]

"As the front moved southward, the Germans stubbornly gave little ground. A stronghold at St. Lo held our movement at bay requiring the Allied Air Force to level it to the ground. This called for a holding pattern while the strategists planned our next move. This new strategy would not unfold for months which gave our company time to settle into a camp site for the balance of June and move southward towards St. Lo. American Armor and Infantry opened a corridor isolating parts of Brittany as they had already sealed off Cherbourg on the Colentin Peninsula. Meanwhile, in mid-August, Hitler, refusing to authorize a retreat, began to show his weakness when nearly one hundred thousand German soldiers were surrounded and captured at what is now known as the Falaise Gap.

"The strategists had planned the maneuver with concern for the lives of troops by waiting to encircle this large concentration of German divisions. That is when the Third Army began to move eastward with the Germans in full retreat which many believe was the turning point in the liberation of Paris.

GRACE UNDER FIRE?

"I wish to write of an incident that happened in Normandy sometime during our holdover between June and July. The Army Special Services were showing movies in the area and notice was given that one would be shown at twilight just a short distance up the lane. 'Twilight' in mid-June in France is a misnomer because it did not become dark at that latitude until about 10 p.m. In any event, the starting time was late by civilian standards and it was a short walk measuring about a mile from camp to the movie venue. There were large poles supporting camouflage nets under which a movie projector had been set up encircled by troops of the area. It was less than a minute into the showing when shouts rang out, 'GAS! GAS!'

"Assuming that the movie venue would be a short distance from camp, we had neglected to bring our gasmasks. Mistake number one. My first impulse was to climb a tree reasoning that gas being heavier than air would stay at ground level. Nevertheless, my instinct was to return to camp as quickly as possible, which I did.

"What happened in the ensuing minutes brought me to a new stage of maturity. As I hastened back to camp along the shaded lane with a prayer on my lips, I learned more during that brief incident about human nature than at any period in my lifetime. I saw bravery and self-control and, sadly, witnessed cowardice. As our trucks were dispatched to retrieve us, overcrowding, pushing, and shoving of one's friends and comrades was not a pretty sight to see. One soldier, in particular, who during training styled himself as a model of perfection, showed his true colors as a whining coward. He was reminded of his conduct in the many months that followed and was never accepted as being dependable in time of crisis from then on.

"What intrigued me about this gas incident was that cattle were seen grazing in the meadow nearby under no apparent harm or distress. That is when my fears were calmed knowing that cattle breathe air as we do.

"Ironically, the upshot of the story was that there was no gas attack. Someone returning from a gasoline depot on that hot summer day noticed that the litmus tape on the hood of his truck had turned red. The Army star on each vehicle had special litmus tape applied to it to provide a warning in the presence of gas. The chemical reaction to the gas fumes from the gas depot was mistaken for evidence of a gas attack.

"The struggle to move deeper into France was one small skirmish after another. Field by field, town by town, we fought on from our landing in June to the 18th of July when St. Lo finally fell. While all of this was going on, many battalions held their positions, waiting for the breakthrough that was in the process of developing. Heading south under the cover of darkness, we had to thread through a narrow corridor to Avranches, Rennes and then east to the Leval-Lemans Crossing. With German resistance on both our flanks, the skies were lit with thunderous cannon and mortar fire. A display beyond my wildest imagination was taking place before my eyes. As morning light showed evidence of pluses and minuses, the Germans had suffered the greater loss. Their Armored units were ablaze in scattered remnants of what was once a great fighting machine. Also, an unexpected revelation of improbability was that the cannon and mortar fire concussion had thrown nine hundred-pound cows twenty feet up in the air and lodged them onto tree branches. By some estimates, animals that were killed by mines and artillery fire ran into the hundreds.

"Under the command of General George Patton's Third Army, the breakthrough came by surrounding and then capturing thousands of German troops at the Falaise Gap. Meanwhile, our company attached to the XX Corps continued south to the Level-Lemans Crossing. Our company was moving eastward at a rate of forty miles a day onto Orléans throughout the month of August.

THE ATROCITIES OF THE NAZI REGIME

"After making a crossing at the Meuse River and then setting up Headquarters in Metz in the month of October and early November, it was time for some rest and repairs to our equipment. A disturbing memory of human suffering still haunts me today of a scene I witnessed in Metz during chowtime. After we discarded our meal's leftovers into the garbage cans, a very old lady and children of toddler age reached into the garbage cans to gather our leavings to eat. This tugged at our heartstrings so that we gave up some of our unsoiled food and offered some of our C-Rations. Sights such as these during my wartime experience molded within me a conservative approach to life. Not to be misunderstood, a conservative back in the 40s was described as a person of a frugal nature, one who conserves and who is not wasteful. I make that distinction so as not to confuse the term with the political connotation.

"Another example of human deprivation caused by the conflict of war occurred when a farmer on a horse drawn wagon triggered a land mine in a meadow. The farmer was knocked unconscious, but the horse was fatally wounded. Before the farmer could regain consciousness, people began to gather seemingly coming from nowhere. Whether by consent or bargain, they began butchering the horse where it lay. In a very short time, all that remained was a carcass and a turned over wagon. Such was the shortage of food and the never-ending will to survive in a crisis environment. There was so much human suffering due to famine that it drove many to compromise their morals doing what they must just to survive. This sadly was the reality of the conflict between the human animal and the law of the jungle in pursuit of self-preservation.

"As we drove deeper into Germany, to our horror we witnessed the true cruelty which revealed the full depravity of Hitler's Third Reich. Even though hardened by months of battle, we were aghast at the conditions to which these poor souls were subjected in this hell called a prison camp. Bodies were piled in heaps and those who survived were little more than skin drawn over their bones. Men who at one point in time weighed some 165 pounds were now emaciated to walking skeletons. The Stars and Stripes, the Armed Forces newspaper, reported in an April edition, that the British had freed from a Belsen concentration camp, 55,000 still alive. In addition, hundreds of thousands of dead awaited cremation. A foul odor permeated our camp that remained in my senses for several days after this experience.[xvi]

"These scenes filled the troops with a cold anger, while everywhere German civilians insisted, they knew nothing of these atrocities ever having taken place. TO THE READERS OF THIS TEXT, PLEASE NOTE THAT AS YEARS PASS THAT MANY WILL DENY THAT SUCH ATROCITIES AS THE HOLOCAUST EVER TOOK PLACE. BELIEVE ME, I SAW THE WASTED

BODIES OF THOUSANDS STACKED LIKE CORDWOOD. NEVER EVER BELIEVE THE DENIALS OF THOSE WHO WISH TO CLEANSE THE PAST OF THEIR MISDEEDS.

CHRISTMAS EVE, 1944

"At this point in the war, it was my job along with buddy, John Strohm, to service and maintain large construction equipment, such as sixteen ton bulldozers, road graders, and power shovels. With these construction units scattered around the countryside, it was up to us to locate them and get them in running condition. We were issued maps of the reported locations and made every effort to reach them for service and repairs.

"There were times when we managed to get lost in unfamiliar areas. Once in particular, when the Battle of the Bulge was being defended further north from our position, we headed south in search of a piece of equipment. In so doing, we lost our way and with dark closing in, we decided to settle down for the night in an old farmhouse in the middle of nowhere. It had been snowing during the day with an accumulation nearing a foot deep, so we decided to layover for the night.

"We built a fire to stay warm and melted snow for coffee. After eating our dinner rations, we made plans for alternating shifts for the night watch. While we were enjoying our coffee, Johnny looked over his coffee mug and said, 'Merry Christmas, Blackie!' We spent Christmas Eve of 1944 in an old farmhouse deep in the heart of Germany.

"Remembering what I did that Christmas Eve does not tax my memory for it is fresh in my mind still fifty years later. At the break of dawn, we surveyed the area around the farmhouse. Johnny Strohm and I were working on a Coleman Crane in a place called Strasbourg, Germany. The use of this crane was for the unloading of fifty-gallon oil drums used to create clouds of smoke which would give ground cover to our troops' activities. The Germans were very proficient in their artillery skills and putting up a curtain of smoke over and around our position reduced their accuracy. After some time on the front line, one could distinguish their incoming from *outgoing shells. Ours seemed to swish as opposed to theirs which gave out a wobbling sound.*

"*Johnny was working on the motor section of the crane, and my toolbox was on the ground near the back end. While making a selection of a wrench I needed, Johnny called for assistance at the front. I had just left the rear of this large piece of equipment and climbed up on the cab when a thunderous explosion lifted and rocked the rear end of the crane. It was a direct hit of either a mortar or artillery shell that struck and blew out eight tires of four feet in diameter to shreds. Had I still been standing there at the rear of the truck, I would not have survived that blast. To this day, whenever I get down on myself, I remember the reprieve that God so generously gave to me.*

"*Another memory of Johnny that continues to endear him to me comes from a time when we were out in the French countryside attempting to locate a vehicle in need of repair. Hungry and needing a break, we were preparing to stop for some chow from our C-rations. Spotting a garden by an abandoned house, I saw what was easily familiar to me as potato plants, so I started digging. Johnny looked at me as though I had lost my mind, 'What are you doin', Blackie?' As I triumphantly pulled out a string of spuds hung on a tangle of roots, I exclaimed, 'We're gonna have baked potatoes!' Johnny was incredulous as I packed several of them in mud and threw them into a small cooking fire we had built. In no time, we had hot baked potatoes for our supper. 'Well, I'll be,' exclaimed Johnny, the boy from New York City. 'And here I thought that potatoes grew on trees!'*

THE DRIVE TO THE RHINE

"*The Allies frontal push was moving at a pace far greater than logistics could supply the mechanized units to the point that Patton's tanks could not be adequately supplied with gasoline. Our company, also on the move, was running the gauntlet with depleting gas supplies. Out of necessity, we had to layover in Verdun, a battlefield of World War I fame.*

"As a boy, I recall seeing a movie starring Jimmy Cagney, a war film about the Fighting 69th. The scene was to have taken place in this field of conflict. Now with some reflection, I tried to recreate in my mind this historic event of twenty-seven years ago. Had we not learned anything from past history? Clearly from where I stood, the adage paraphrased by Winston Churchill could not have been more appropriate: 'Those who fail to learn from history are condemned to repeat it.'

"Easter Sunday of 1945, much like Christmas of 1944, remains clear to me even fifty years later. It was the crossing of the Rhine River at Mainx. On that Easter Sunday at 12:30 a.m., I drove a large Army truck across a floating pontoon bridge measuring some fifteen hundred feet in length. History records how the Germans' failure to blow up the Remagen Bridge may have contributed to a positive turning point in the war for the Allies and setback for Hitler. However, before the Remagen prize was ever conceived a possibility, Army strategists had planned a crossing south of Remagen by laying a pontoon bridge across the Rhine. The pontoon bridge was built by the Army Corps of Engineers and it is with pride that our company shared with some measure of participation. Although I believe that this pontoon bridge was the longest ever built, there is no mention of it in the Guinness Book of World Records. I believe with all my heart that it is worthy of note especially because it was constructed under wartime conditions.

"The war began to take on a more certain turn of positive events as we, the Third Army, continued to move eastward to the city of Frankfurt, Eisenach, and the concentration camp of Buchenwald. The German forces were now in full retreat and talk of surrender with a settlement for peace was now closer to reality than just a mere hope. We then began to move to a more southerly direction on towards Austria along the Bohemian Forest. Settling in an area called Lambach, we were billeted in a palatial compound where Lipizzaner[xvii] show horses were bred and trained. This was a period of time with less confrontation in a more relaxed atmosphere. It allowed us time to restore our fragile emotions diverted by playing baseball and other forms of recreational activities.

"The ending of the war was in full evidence when German armies began surrendering en masse. I could have been credited, as were many in my company, with citations for capturing entire German companies who were, in fact, giving themselves up in surrender. That, to me, would have been a farce on my military record and conscience. Sadly, however, many took full advantage of what we referred to as 'Cracker Jack commendations' by accepting Bronze Stars that were not deserved. In my view, it makes a mockery of those who were wounded in action and others who died so nobly in defense of their beloved country. To accept awards without merit disrespects the brave veterans who performed above and beyond the call of duty.

"The war in Europe came to an end on May 8, 1945, however, the cessation of conflict gave no reason to relax military discipline. We continued to function as a unit. Proper appearance was demanded along with respect for rank and authority. As we began moving westward, the war with Japan was still to be resolved. Leaving Austria in late May, our unit began retracing fairly closely to the route we had taken months earlier. We stopped occasionally in places named Salzburg, Munich, and Stuttgart, then turning southward to Nancy, Dijon and finally the seaport of Marseilles in southeastern France. It was estimated that we traveled about 800 miles. While in Marseilles, we serviced our equipment and made ready for our next move through the Suez Canal, destination–Calcutta.

"But all this preparation was halted when the atom bomb was dropped on Japan on August 6th whereupon the Japanese soon surrendered and sued for peace on August 12, 1945. With this fortunate turn of events, it wasn't long before our unit made ready to be shipped back to the States. Our ship, the S.S. General Harry Taylor, sailed up the Hudson River with all the pomp and circumstance befitting a royal welcome. There were boats spraying plumes of water high in the air and the feeling of euphoria was widespread. We were trucked to Camp Shanks and treated royally again for three days. Boarding troop trains, we were transported to Fort Devens, Massachusetts whereupon I was processed and discharged on October 25, 1945.

"I can in no way relate every incident that I experienced accurately from March 3, 1943 to October 25, 1945 for it would take reams of paper to be put into book form as was not my intention."[xviii]

Even though it seems that it was not Dad's intention that his military memoirs be published, I believe he would be pleased and proud to know that his first person account of his military experiences was recognized by António Fragoeiro, a researcher of the military history of Portugal and the Portuguese during World War II, 1939-1945. An article authored by Fragoeiro containing excerpts from Dad's memoirs and photos that he took himself, were published in the June, 2023 issue of *Revista Portuguesa de História Militar*, "Jorge Rei—Relato e Memórias de um Lusodescendente."

AFTERMATH

Like many World War II veterans, my father did not speak of his experiences during the war for many years but there is no doubt that his time in the service changed him forever. There always seemed to be a tension about him like a tightly wound coil that is ready to spring at any moment. He had a dislike of travel to the point that I was ten years of age before we crossed the state line from Rhode Island for a day trip to see the Plymouth Rock, the Mayflower, and Plymouth Plantations in Massachusetts. We never took a family vacation in all my years at home. When I asked him why we never traveled anywhere, he told me that he promised himself during the war that if he ever got out of there alive, he would never leave home again. In later years after I was married, we enjoyed several family trips together to Disney World with the grandsons, to southwest Virginia to visit the Fraleys, and to Nantucket Island, but only because my husband, Dave, and I planned all the logistics where he and Mom needed only to come along and enjoy the ride.

If he ever felt the symptoms of PTSD, he would not have let on to us because the manly thing to do from his perspective would be to "tough it out." Nevertheless, there seemed to me to be a struggle going on within him because, while he did not speak of the war, he certainly watched every World War II movie that appeared on television. At the time near the end of the war, when his unit arrived at Hitler's "Eagle's Nest" in Berchtesgaden, Germany, he picked up several Nazi artifacts for souvenirs like many of the soldiers did. I recall a full-sized Nazi flag, Nazi insignia, a couple of bayonets and a few other items that he kept tucked away until one day, he saw an ad in the local paper placed by a dealer seeking WWII memorabilia. I remember the day that the dealer came to the house to see what Dad had to offer. As he examined the collection spread out on the living room floor, the dealer asked, "How much do you want for all of it?" I heard my father say, "Just take it. I'm done with the war."

It was fifty years later that he finally wrote down his memories vowing that he would not write about the "gross" stuff. I have no doubt that he has offered only a sanitized version of whatever he experienced. Although I know most certainly that he was a true patriot who was proud of his service to his country, I believe that this writing project was part of his process to discover where his part fit into the grander scheme of history in order to satisfy himself that it was ultimately worth it.

The following was found among Dad's notes, although he does not claim authorship nor witness to the experience.

> *"I REMEMBER WELL: A soldier in the field of battle, in an anguished wounded moment, was heard to say, 'Gee, I didn't even hear the bullet' and mercifully passed away."*

MEDALS, BADGES, AND INSIGNIA

LEGEND: MILITARY DISPLAY

JOSEPH RAY, U.S. ARMY Serial #: 31 291 050
Grade at Discharge: TEC 4 Sergeant
Organization: 623rd Engineer Light Equipment Company
Dates of Service: March 3, 1943 (induction)–October 25, 1945 (discharge)
Military Occupation: Automotive Mechanic

PHOTO: PVT Joseph Ray (1943 prior to deployment to Europe)

MEDAL: WWII European-African-Middle Eastern Campaign Medal (Purchased New in 2020 as these were not struck until 1947)

"The European-African-Middle Eastern Campaign Medal (EAMECM) is a military award that recognizes the service of U.S. Armed Forces personnel who performed military duty in the European Theatre during World War II. Created on November 6, 1942 by President Franklin D. Roosevelt's Executive Order 9265 it was originally just a ribbon and there was not a full-sized medal until 1947. The first recipient of the medal was General of the Army Dwight Eisenhower."

MEDAL: Good Conduct Medal (Original)

DOG TAGS: (Original)

CAMPAIGN RIBBONS:
- European-African-Middle Eastern Campaign Medal Ribbon with 5 Black Stars denoting each of the Campaigns served: 1) Normandy, 2) Ardennes, 3) Northern France, 4) Central Europe, 5) Rhineland (Original)
- Good Conduct Medal Ribbon (Original)

LAPEL PINS:
- World War II Honorable Discharge "Ruptured Duck" Lapel Pin (Original)
- Good Conduct Medal Lapel Pin (Original)

COLLAR PINS:
- Brass U.S. Collar Device Pin (Original)
- Brass U.S. Army Corps of Engineers Collar Device Pin (Original)

PATCHES:
- First Army Patch: Black Block "A"—reassigned (Original)
- Third Army Patch: White "A" in red circle—first assignment (Original with added "Dog Tag Chain" embellishment) then unit returned to Third Army
- World War II Victory Patch (Purchased new in 2020)
- Tech 4 Stripes Patches for WWII (Original)

- Four Gold Bars Sleeve Patch: Each bar signifies 6 months of overseas service therefore four bars equal two years served (Original)
- World War II Honorable Discharge Regulation Patch: Gold "Ruptured Duck" in Gold Circle: "Worn above the right breast pocket by Army personnel having been Honorably Discharged from the service in WWII. It allowed the uniform to be worn for 30 days after discharge due to the civilian clothing shortage and also indicated that the soldier was not AWOL." (Original)

NOTE: Marie Fraley, daughter of Sgt. Ray, found his WWII army uniform among his things with all original patches and insignia intact. He wore a size 31" waist / 33" inseam pants, 36R jacket and shirt with 14 ½" collar and 32" sleeve. Too molded and moth-eaten to save, the wool uniform was discarded but the patches and insignia were removed and mounted in this memory box.

Found in the breast pocket of his uniform jacket was a white tissue with a lipstick blot saved all those years. Dad said it was a token from an "English rose" wishing the "Yank" luck while waiting in England for the call for the D-Day invasion.

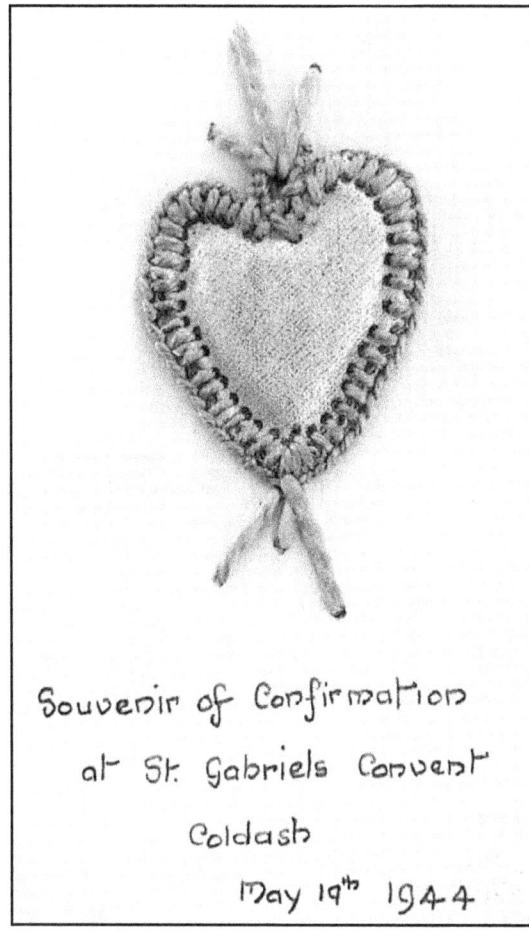 

While preparing for D-Day in England, George took the opportunity to receive the sacrament of Confirmation on May 19, 1944 at St. Gabriel's Convent, Coldash. He kept the souvenir throughout the war and it remains among his mementos.

(Left) Written on back: "Agnus Dei—piece of wax stamped with the image of the Lamb of God and blessed by the Pope every 7th year of his reign."

(Above right) The Military Missal of PVT Joseph Ray carried with him throughout World War II was found among his memorabilia, well-thumbed but still in good condition 75 years later.

MILITARY PHOTO ALBUM

BASIC TRAINING: CAMP SHELBY, MISSISSIPPI, MARCH–DECEMBER, 1943

(1) PVT Joseph Ray; (2) PVT Herbert Long, PVT Joseph Ray;
(3) PVT Gates, PVT Donald Rich, PVT Joseph Ray

PVT Joseph Ray (far left), others unidentified

CAMP SHANKS, STAGING AREA, DECEMBER, 1943

Taken at a nightclub in New York City while stationed at Camp Shanks, New York, the staging area for deployment overseas to Europe. The unit departed New York City port on 9 January, 1944 aboard the Santa Barbara[xix] arriving in Liverpool, England on 20 January 1945.

(L-R) PVT Edward Picard and PVT Joseph Ray (both of Phenix, West Warwick, RI) and PVT Lionel LePage and PVT Donald Rich (both of Berlin, NH)

ENGLAND, JANUARY 21–JUNE 21, 1944

Between January and June, 1994 prior to D-Day, the 623rd Engineer Light Equipment Company was engaged in several projects in the Wokingham area requiring the much needed earth moving equipment that the U.S. troops transported to Europe with them. Among

CPL Joseph Ray manning a bulldozer in England prior to D-Day.

those projects was the construction of the Royal Navy Air Field near Abbington which had suffered continual delays due to equipment repairs "75% of the time" with the local contractors who could not obtain necessary parts.[xx]

FRANCE, JUNE 23, 1944–MARCH 20, 1945

The participation of the 623rd Engineer Light Equipment Infantry Company with the Third Army in the Normandy and Northern France Campaigns took place over nine months from the landing on Omaha Beach near Trévières to Metz. Twenty motor marches of over 700 miles are documented.[xxi]

(1) "G. P. Truck" or General Purpose Truck was used for making repairs out in the field. "Boom on the front was used to lift motors from other vehicles. It was equipped with a full assortment of tools, a lathe, and drills. It was a machine shop on wheels." JGR

(2) (L-R) Joseph Ray, DiMarche, Red McDonough in Metz, France, November, 1944.

(3) (L-R) W.B. Klarke, ? Shuzt, Joseph Ray in France. The photo was sent home and stamped on back "For Personal Use Only, Not For Publication, 18 Dec 1944, Theatre Censor ? USA."

GERMANY, MARCH 20, 1945–MAY 4, 1945

From Huttersdorf to Vilshofen, on the Austrian border, the unit participated in the Rhineland Campaign covering approximately 900 miles in seventeen motor marches.[xxii] The photos taken below are identified by SGT Ray as *"on convoy somewhere in Germany."*

(L–R) (1) SGT Ray washing out of his helmet "still with soap on my face."
(2) "Helping cook peel potatoes."
(3) "Checking what needs to be checked."

AUSTRIA, MAY 5–JUNE 20, 1945

It was while in Lambach, Austria at the end of the war that the unit was able to step foot in Hitler's "Eagle's Nest," the *Kehlsteinhaus*, in Berchtesgarden, Germany following its destruction. Bombed by the 8th Air Force, the residence had an 80 foot silo with an elevator which Hitler could ascend to look out over the Alps and the countryside. There were many Nazi artifacts left behind which the soldiers took as souvenirs.

Remains of Hilter's "Eagle's Nest" following bombing at end of the war.
(These photos were taken by SGT Ray.)

(1) View of the Alps from Hitler's Eagle's Nest with top brass in the foreground during press event (note PRESS sign on jeep).

(2) SGT Ray posing with props found at the Eagle's Nest. This unique photo shows an oversized replica of The Cross of Honor of the German Mother, or Mutterkreuz, awarded by the German Reich to mothers who "exhibited probity, exemplary motherhood, and who conceived and raised at least four or more children in the role of a parent."[xxiii]

SGT Ray showing off an accordion he found in an abandoned farmhouse in Austria at the end of the war. He said that since he could not play it, he gave it to another soldier who could.

GERMANY–FRANCE, JUNE 20–SEPTEMBER 3, 1945

Returning west through Germany to France, the unit pushed for over 1,175 miles to the staging area in Calas, France. The unit remained there for about three weeks giving the troops an opportunity for R & R in Paris before shipping stateside from Marseille on September 3 aboard the USS General Taylor.[xxiv]

SGT Ray in Paris in front of L'Arc de Triomphe; Eiffel Tower.

(Left) PVT Joseph Ray, March 1943, Camp Shelby, Mississippi, (Right) T/SGT Joseph Ray, March 8, 1945, Austria.

Part Three:
Family Life

HOME AGAIN, HOME AGAIN

Honorably discharged from the U.S. Army on October 25, 1945, George returned home to the little house on Wakefield Street. Like many returning servicemen, it must have seemed strange to be back. The house was the same, the neighborhood was the same, but he was no longer the impressionable youth who left home in March of 1943. Within those thirty months, he had seen and experienced unimaginable suffering, death, atrocities, and destruction in places that he had never expected to set foot. He was a changed man. One need only to compare the "before photo" of the smiling callow recruit during basic training in 1943 with the "after photo" of the seasoned soldier in Austria in 1945 at the end of the war to grasp the impact of that experience.

His brother, Alfred, was discharged at about the same time, but Frankie was still serving for a few more months until April of 1946. Frankie would return to his wife, Fernande, when he was discharged. Tommy and Evelyn were still at home with MaMa and PaPa. It must have been quite an adjustment for everyone to have a full house again. With two grown men at loose ends added to the household, it could not have been easy for anyone. Tommy, still at home and too young to serve in this war, recalled an argument in the house between two of the brothers that turned physical to the point that their father intervened to break it up. Tommy remembers his father holding them apart and yelling, "You two have been to hell and back and you come home to fight each other? You're brothers!" Grown war-hardened men as they were, Frank Ray could still keep his boys in line.

There were quieter grounding moments as well. One touching poem penned by George recollects his experience while visiting the local variety store in the neighborhood after the war. It is a simple but poignant memory that re-centered him by transporting him back to his childhood while demonstrating all too clearly just how far he had come since those days.

DÉJÀ VU ALL OVER AGAIN

In a small section of town,
Where I'll begin my story,
There was a little place to buy candy,
Owned by a man called Charlie Murray.
Penny candy was sold there,
Along with bread and such staples,
In addition to sundry things,
You could purchase the daily paper.

The candy counter at Murray's,
Was long and fronted with glass,
And when making a choice of candy,
It better be something that lasts.
I ran my gaze along the glass case,
Viewing candy from end to end,
Perusing these large assortments,
With little money to spend.

Still searching this long candy counter,
With a choice I was not yet shown,

Part Three: Family Life

A kindly stranger said to Charlie,
Give the kid a big ice cream cone.
As I stood in silent amazement,
That this stranger had purchased for me,
Such a giant sized ice cream cone,
Lives long in my memory.

Now many years have passed,
As a grown man returned home from war,
I was surprised how little had changed,
At Murray's candy and variety store.
To again see this center of activity,
And remembering how it was then,
I bought a giant ice cream cone for a kid,
As I thought to myself,
"My God, It's like déjà vu, all over again!" *

– Joseph "George" Ray, December, 1993

* "It's like déjà vu all over again!" is a quote attributed to Yogi Berra, New York Yankees Hall of Famer, who was as well-known for mangling the English language as he was for his skill on the baseball diamond. His quips are memorable because they often made people laugh or contained enough truth that they made sense.

Dad wrote or said little about that time of limbo, about what it was like to not only settle into this new reality but to try to figure out "What next?" With a surplus of manpower flooding the job market after the war, opportunities for employment were in short supply. Shifting from a wartime economy to a peacetime economy meant changes for everyone.

He did say that he went from job to job until finally landing a position as an apprentice lace weaver in 1946 at Valley Lace Company in Hope, RI. Also known as "twist-hands," lace weavers were highly trained and skilled workers who had to produce the most refined textile products on dirty, loud, and cumbersome machines. It was a good paying job when there were orders to be filled. George landed the job thanks to his uncle,

Joe Furtado Pacheco (he later dropped the Pacheco) who broke the glass ceiling for the Portuguese in the valley to be employed as lace weavers. Previously the sole realm of the English who imported the trade to the northeastern United States, the Portuguese were thought "not smart enough" to do the job. Ironically, all four of the Ray brothers eventually became lace weavers. (More about this in Section Four: The Lace Trade.)

As the months went on, my mother, Mary Lillian Furtado, caught my father's eye. The feeling must have been mutual because they dated for a while. It is not clear how they met, but it is known that George was good friends with Mary's older brother, Danny. Certainly, everyone knew everyone in that community.

As they dated, George was a frequent visitor as he came calling at Mary's house, but he said that after a while he began to feel unwelcome. So he stopped coming around, much to my mother's disappointment. Danny took it upon himself to intervene for his sister taking George aside, "I have to ask you: Do you love my sister? Because if you do, then I wish you'd go see her and propose, because I'm getting sick of hearing her cry!" Before he realized it, George was in the car and parked in the Furtados' driveway. George and Mary had a long talk. On June 28, 1947, they were married at St. Anthony's Church in River Point, Rhode Island.

Wedding portrait of Mary Furtado Ray and Joseph George Ray.

On the steps of St. Anthony's Church (L-R) Eileen Furtado (Maid of Honor and sister of Bride), Mary Furtado Ray, Joseph George Ray, Thomas Ray (Best Man and brother of the Groom), June 28, 1947.

MARRIED LIFE

George and Mary Ray began their married life on 20 Vine Street in a tenement apartment house owned by Mary's father, *Luiz Furtado Couto* / Louis Furtado. *Luiz* had immigrated to the United States in 1915, native of the *Matriz* in *Vila Franca do Campo* on the island of *São Miguel*. He and *Maria da Conceição Simas*, native of *São Pedro* in *Vila Franca do Campo*, met in West Warwick and married in 1920 at SS Peter and Paul Church. They made a life in the small mill town raising four surviving children: Daniel William (b. 1921), Mary Lillian (b. 1922), Louis Emanuel (b. 1924), and Eileen Elizabeth (née Idalina b. 1930). A fifth child, John (b. 1926-d. 1927) passed away at fifteen months of age from croup.

Luiz was illiterate but an excellent brick mason working in construction. In addition to the duplex that he and Maria bought on Coogan's Court for themselves, they purchased two tenement apartment buildings on Vine Street, an easy walk in proximity across the railroad tracks, that he renovated and maintained for rental income. Both sisters Mary and Eileen started their married lives in those apartments that their father remodeled just for them.

George had the greatest respect and admiration for his father-in-law. He said that it was always a great pleasure to work alongside him when helping him make repairs and renovations on the property. He learned much from him with his quiet and patient manner of working out problems. George was most in awe of his father-in-law's ability to walk a roofline thirty feet in the air while repairing chimneys. George, himself prone to vertigo, said, "*Meu Sogro* (my father-in-law), how do you walk up here without getting dizzy?" *Luiz* replied with a smile, "Don't look down, George! Don't look down!"

Luiz and *Maria da Conceição* worked hard and made a good life for themselves and their children through the Great Depression and World War II without the support of the family that they left behind in *São Miguel*. *Maria Conceição* was a strong, resourceful, and reserved woman who was literate in Portuguese. Consequently, she kept up a close correspondence with her sister. *Barbara do Canto*, in "*as ilhas*" ("the islands" as the Azores were called), which laid the foundation for me and my *madrinha* (godmother), Eileen, to reconnect with our roots for the first time on our trip to the homeland in October, 2001.

George and Mary Ray lived in the apartment at 20 Vine Street from the time of their wedding in 1947 until September, 1955. My mother continued to work at the Clyde Print Works in the early years of marriage until morning sickness, which she described as "all day sickness," ended her working career early in 1950. She never worked outside the home again. Their first and only child, Marie Elizabeth, was born on September 3, 1950 at the Lying-In Hospital in Providence.

Our residence is shown as the upper apartment at 20 Vine Street with Marie in front at 3 ½ years of age.

FATHERHOOD

There has never been any doubt in my mind that I was well-loved and cared for by both my mother and my father. While my mother says that I was most definitely wanted, I feel that there was a reason that it was three years after marriage before I was born. To this day, I believe that my father wanted to establish a stable financial base before adding to the family. The fact that I am an only child was intentional to ensure that any children brought forth would be well provided for. It was a point driven home in conversations on our front porch with the parish priest regarding Dad's disagreement with the church's stand on birth control. In fact, a savings account was started specifically for my college education shortly after I was born. Dad departed from the prevailing Portuguese attitude that working to earn money was more important than spending money on an education. He was determined that I would have the education and opportunities that he never had, even if I was a girl.

I remember our first home on 20 Vine Street through specific flashes of memory with my father. It is amazing to me how a child so young can imprint such scenes to mind that have survived the passage of time even until this day. These are highlighted to illustrate the kind of loving father that he was.

One of my earliest memories comes from about the age of about twenty-four months. My father had fashioned a swing out of an old chair so that it would have a back and arms as well as a deep seat and hung it from a low tree branch in the upper yard. He used an old leather belt for my waist, safe enough for a toddler in those days (nothing like the five-point harnesses required today). My father would push me on the swing which I called the "crink" because of the metal-on-metal sound of the chain squeaking with the swing's to-and-fro motion. I remember the movement would lull me to sleep with the dappled sunlight dancing behind my eyelids. He'd let the swing wind down to a stop when, ever-so-gently, he'd lift me up in his arms with my head nestled in the crook of his neck. I recall being in that half-conscious, in-and-out state of dozing, when no sooner had he crossed the threshold of the back door, than I snapped awake and cried, "Crink!" to be pushed again. What parent hasn't thought they were home free with a little one asleep only to have to return to another attempt at the strategy that would finally bring slumber and a break?

Another early memory emerges from about the age of sixteen months when I was given my first tricycle. It was dark blue and white, and brand new. My parents were so excited to give it to me because they had never had anything like it themselves as children. I recall my father placing me on the seat and leaning me forward to put my little hands on the handlebar grips. Leaning over me, he pushed from the back. "Hold on, Marie!" he said in my ear. My legs were too short to reach the pedals but I remember looking down watching them go around and around as we moved along the concrete walkway. Dad, who was always the problem-solver, fashioned blocks of wood with bolts to build up the pedals so I could finally reach them and learn how to pedal the trike myself. He was always providing bridges for me so that I could eventually learn to do things for myself.

Another bicycle moment came at the age of eight, when I received a brand new English bicycle for my birthday. He took me to the grassy athletic field, so that when I fell off it (as was inevitable), I wouldn't fall hard on a concrete sidewalk. There was plenty of space for him to run beside me with his hand on the back of the seat pushing me along until I found my balance and was on my own! Still a young man at thirty-four years of age and reasonably fit, I still hear him huffing and puffing beside me until he felt he could let go, stop running and catch his breath. It was one of those many moments when he was as happy and excited as I was over my accomplishment.

There was never any doubt that Dad took good care of his family, both financially and practically. An example comes to mind while we were still living on 20 Vine Street when hurricane Carol was upon us. It was September of 1954 and the early warning system was already broadcasting the storm's track. Having been caught by surprise, yet surviving the Hurricane of 1938 as a boy, my father was serious about making preparations. Now dependent on electricity for refrigeration, he knew that days without electrical power would cause hardship. Only four years of age, I clearly recall my father digging a deep hole in the ground in the garden near the back door where he placed a cooler with the milk bottle and some perishable foods.

Hurricane Carol is reported to have been one of the worst to hit New England at that time, so much that its name was retired by the National Oceanic and Atmospheric Administration (NOAA).[xxv] Reaching gusts of up to 125 mph in Rhode Island, I recall watching from a bedroom window as tall trees swayed violently and bent to the ground while shingles and debris flew through the air. While I never felt unsafe, later a dead cat was found in the flower garden near the makeshift groundfridge making me realize for the first time just how merciless and dangerous Mother Nature could be.

NO PETS ALLOWED

For some reason, my mother had an aversion to animals. She said that her family had a pet dog in her youth named "Tippy" but that it growled and snapped at her once leaving her forever afraid of animals after that experience. Consequently, between her fear and the mess it would cause in her house, I never had a pet as a child. Until one day, my father was ambushed.

Shortly after Easter I'd been out with the neighborhood kids, quite far from home for me, when we came across someone outside of a tenement house in River Point with a box of baby chicks. Obviously an Easter novelty, the chicks were now unwanted and were going to be destroyed, so I ended up with a baby chick to bring home. Picture a little girl cradling a frail matted, half-dead chick in her chubby hands appealing to her daddy to "fix it." As disciplined as he was, Dad was a softy when it came to being a good Samaritan and appeasing me.

My mother was aghast insisting that she didn't want "that thing" in her house, but Dad loved a challenge and would not disappoint me. He found a small box, lined it with newspaper, and found a lamp to hang above it for warmth as a makeshift brooder. His experience raising chickens on Wakefield Street came in handy but did not prepare him for nursing a sickly chicken back to health. Recognizing what is now called "a teachable moment," Dad taught me how to feed the chick with an eyedropper, later mashing up crackers to feed it, and how to change the paper frequently. So what are you going to name it? "Angela!" I said, thinking it was an angel with wings that had come back to life.

Thanks to Dad's (and my) care in the "chick ICU," Angela perked up, improved, and began to grow shedding its down and sprouting feathers. Soon it was too large for the little box and needed a much larger box in the basement. In no time, it was fully grown, jumping out of the box, running around the basement making a mess and...crowing! Angela was not a hen after all—it was a rooster! My pet, now dubbed "Angelo," had exhausted my mother's patience and he had to go. Moreover, it did not make for a cuddly pet by any stretch of the imagination. It's hard to love a chicken.

Lucky for Angelo, my Vovô Ray still had his chicken coop at the house on Wakefield Street, so Angelo was summarily evicted and relocated. What transpired next is a lesson in social engineering. It seems that in keeping Angelo isolated as a pet in our basement, he had missed the critical learning stage of socialization and had not developed the skills to be a well-adjusted rooster. My grandfather reported that his assimilation into the culture of the hen house was going poorly. He didn't know how to behave like a rooster and the hens were chasing and abusing him. He was literally "hen pecked." Ultimately, Vovô had no choice but to sacrifice Angelo to Sunday dinner to keep the peace in the hen house. I was told that Angelo died of natural causes only learning the truth many years later along with my grandmother's confession, that she could not bring herself to eat that roast chicken dinner.

The moral of the story is that Dad taught me a wonderful lesson in compassion and care, but also that sometimes the best intentions of intervention do not end well in the end...and, that chickens make lousy pets. In memory of Angelo, Dad penned the following taking some poetic license in giving Angelo a much better outcome than was his fate.

METAMORPHOSE A TO O

Easter, that certain time of the year,
That evokes the coming of spring,
When tulips and lilies come alive,
And the melody of birds heard to sing.

When we celebrate a new dawning,
With laughter of children in the air,
The joy of hunting for candy and eggs,
With cuddly bunnies and baby chicks to care.

Soon on a Monday, past Easter,
A sick chick to my home arrives,
To nurse this poor little chick to health,
Is more than I could contrive.

A small wooden box was needed,
And a light bulb so as to heat,
With an eyedropper to feed it,
And newspapers to keep the box neat.

As the days and weeks passed,
Marie would feed and clean her.
She refrained from calling it "Chicky,"
And instead named the bird "Angela."

As Angela grew larger in the box,
And her golden feathers had grown,
The chick was now much too big,
And needed to find a new home.

So we asked for grandfather's help,
To find Angela a new placing,
She was thrown in the coop with strangers,
Where sadly she took a lacing.

But Angela was a fighter,
For a girl bird stood her ground,
As she grew bigger and stronger,
Other chickens did not fool around.

So on a bright sunrise morning,
With the sky red and aglow,
Angela had the urge to crow,
That's when Angela, became Angelo!

Now Angelo reigns supreme,
To signal in a new dawning,
The sun will not rise,
Until Angelo signals that it's morning.

MOVING ON UP

By 1955, through their hard work and frugal habits, my parents had saved enough money for a down payment on a home of their own. My mother had spotted an ad in the paper for a pretty Queen Anne dormered house with a pillared front porch for sale on the other side of town. It was in a prime area called "Park Hill" according to the old timers in town. Surrounding houses were owned by doctors, lawyers, and local businessmen. In fact, the house on 50 Greene Street had been built in 1930 by a local lawyer who became town solicitor and, ultimately, a family court judge.

It was nicely situated on a knoll on a double lot facing east. The interior was a three bedroom, one bath, center hall colonial with formal living and dining room, study with

Part Three: Family Life

built-in bookcases, hardwood floors and beautiful woodwork. It was traditional, classic and just exactly to my mother's taste. The lawyer had built a brick contemporary ranch diagonally across the street in 1948, so therefore sold the house to a Mr. Allison and family, he, the manager of the Sears & Roebuck Store in Arctic, the local shopping center.

When Allison was transferred to a Sears store in Presque Isle, Maine in 1955, he put the house on the market. My father began negotiations with Mr. Allison. The asking price was $23,000 which was too high for my father. He made his offer at $18,000 which Ellison turned down saying he had refused $21,000. As time was of the essence for the Allison family to relocate and being under pressure to sell, Allison eventually accepted my father's offer at $18,000. Congratulations to my father for sticking to his price thereby limiting the mortgage to $2,000.

Some years later, my father revealed to me that Allison confided that the lawyer who had originally built the house was not pleased that a Portuguese family was moving into the neighborhood and buying "his" house. He approached Allison with a higher offer saying, "I'll give you $2,000 more than the "Portagee" is giving you." Rumor has it that there was bad blood between the lawyer and Allison, so the offer was soundly refused on principle.

We moved into that house on my fifth birthday, September 3, 1955. It was a comfortable and beautiful home that saw holiday celebrations, my descent down the staircase on my wedding day, and grandsons' Easter egg hunts in the yard. Nevertheless, the bad taste of the ethnic slur remained as a hard reminder of the lowly status of the Portuguese in the pecking order of West Warwick society.

George and Mary were proud of their home and worked hard to maintain and furnish it. My mother's taste ran to dark mahogany traditional furniture and classic fabrics. She chose quality pieces that were the best they could afford, which indeed lasted in excellent condition for almost fifty years, as long as they owned that house. My father maintained the yard and shrubbery himself. He mowed his own lawn and trimmed the foundation shrubs as well as the hedges at the sidewalk in front of the house. At the rear on the backyard boundary with the neighbor's yard, there was a line of arborvitae shrubs that grew to twelve feet high. They had grown together over the years to form a wall all across the back and side of the property. He ingeniously lashed a hedge trimmer to a long bamboo pole to reach the tops and sweep the sides to keep the greenery neat and in line. It was a chore that became a burden once the symptoms of Parkinson's Disease began to emerge. A few times, he enlisted his teenage grandson, Ben, for help with mowing, trimming, and sealing the driveway, probably more as a lesson in the value of hard manual work than for help. For as long as he could, Dad did all the painting, maintenance, and repairs himself believing, as most Portuguese do, that it was a waste of money to pay someone else to do a job you could do yourself.

PLAY IT AGAIN, DAD!

A bonus feature of the house was a finished "rumpus room" in the basement that became my playroom. It could be chilly and damp in the winter but it was the coolest room in the house on the hottest days of summer since the house had no central air conditioning given the era of its construction. Always trying to figure out the best way to give me opportunities, my father found a second hand, upright, player piano for me so that I could take piano lessons. For some reason, my mother did not want it in the living room, probably because it was shabby looking and obviously did not fit in with her décor. So the next logical spot for it was the basement rumpus room.

The living room would have been such an easy move: up the porch stairs, through the wide front door, make the swing in the large foyer and in you go! The basement, however, meant through the back door with a tight double turn and down the basement stairs. It was much too heavy for even four strong men with the right equipment as the metal "harp" itself was extremely weighty; moreover, the case was tall and the legs in one solid wooden "L" shape stuck out.

With a little research, it is learned that an upright piano can weigh between 300 and 500 pounds or more and can have 12,000 individual pieces.[xxvi] As the cited moving.com article advises, "And since you can't exactly take a piano apart and put it back together again just for your move, you'll have to figure out a way to move everything at once…" but George Ray did just that! My father's solution was to take the thing apart—every piece of it including hammers, keys, the guts of the player mechanism, pedals, right back to the soundboard.

It is a vivid memory of mine at the age of about eight, when two of Dad's brothers, Frankie and Alfred, came to his aid and wrestled with that piano. They took it all apart in the garage, numbered the pieces, and sorted them into boxes. The last piece, the case with the "harp" and pinboard bolted to the soundboard, was moved in one piece. When it became clear that the legs were not going to make the turn at the top of the basement stairs, my father's solution was to saw them off at an angle and reattach them later. The large case made it down the stairs with two men on the bottom and one on top. To this day I am amazed that it did not get away from them and careen down the stairs with the force of gravity. Once the case was installed in its place against a wall, my father let his brothers go home with his thanks. His next step was to put the thing back together, which he eventually did exclaiming with pride, "...and not one piece left over!" To which I, in my eight year old naiveté said, "Oh thank you! Now play it!" It was a family joke for years. Certainly if my father could take a piano apart and put it back together, he could play it!

The sad ending of this story is that my three years of piano lessons with the nuns at St. Anthony's convent did not match my father's effort in moving the piano itself. Practicing in the damp rumpus room wearing my coat in the winter was less than enjoyable so I eventually gave it up. When it was necessary for my parents to move to assisted living, the house went on the market with a condition of sale that the piano be left *in situ*. Dad always said that the only way that the piano was going to come out of the basement again was with a sledgehammer and a hack saw.

Unfortunately, the storied Correia musical DNA did not find expression in either of us. I am proud to say, however, that both of George's grandsons are excellent musicians: John on the bass guitar performs with his wife, Melissa (composer, pianist, and musical director) in their group "Minus World" and Ben holds a Doctor of Music in percussion performing often with his wife Jennifer (also Doctor of Music in clarinet) in local orchestras and their own "Sources Duo" videos.

DRIVING WITH DAD

No account of my adolescence would be complete without an anecdote about my patient Dad teaching me how to drive the family car. Fast forward to age fifteen and a half years when I was eligible for a driver's permit in the State of Rhode Island. Having completed my Driver's Education course at the high school with Mr. Gus Olson (the same Gus Olson that taught Dad ninth grade English), I was ready for practical lessons with Dad in a wide open parking lot on Sunday afternoons. We had a sky blue Plymouth Belvedere with automatic transmission operated with push buttons instead of on the column or a gear box on the floor. The car was easy to handle and Dad was patient as I got the feel of the accelerator and the brake.

Next lesson took us out on the back country roads of West Warwick and Cranston. I had a sudden flashback from my childhood of standing up in the back seat at the age of three when my mother froze at the wheel on that same road in the face of an oncoming car in her lane. That latent memory must have been hovering just below consciousness because I was hugging the right side of the road on these narrow country lanes. There was little traffic but I was nervous as cars passed me coming in the opposite direction. "Marie!" Dad exclaimed pushing the steering wheel left as I missed a telephone pole by inches, "You're too far over on the right!" "But the cars are coming toward me on the left!" I lamented. "Marie! Those cars can move but the telephone pole can't!" I could never argue with my father's logic.

GROW OLD WITH ME

George and Mary were happily married for sixty years. I say "happily" with the caveat that they certainly had their share of disagreements as any couple. In those days, couples stayed the course and weathered the rough waters of the hardship of unemployment, and episodes of disappointment. Divorce was last resort in those days and I never heard that word uttered or that concept raised in our home. Over the years, my mother always supported my father in his employment, business, and political efforts, but if she thought he was "out of his mind," she would say so. For my father's part, I have no doubt that my mother was the love of his life and always did his best to care for and protect her. He turned his paycheck in unfailingly for her to manage the household accounts. She was a disciplined saver and he was an astute investor so together they made a good team that secured our financial future far beyond their humble beginnings.

George penned the following poem for my mother one Christmas well into their marriage as he had started the practice of inserting his thoughts in poetry into holiday and birthday cards. After forty-six years of marriage, they had long ago run out of ideas for presents to give each other. As you will see from his "footnote," there was some disagreement between them about the identity of the little girl at the beach outing. Although my mother tended to take things quite literally, it is my belief that whatever beautiful essence that my father saw in that little girl, he found again in my mother. There was never any doubt in my mind of his abiding affection for her over the sixty years that they were married. The birthday poem "Happy Birthday, Mary" says it much better.

A NUMBER TEN IN MY LIFE

In the early turn of the century,
With the coming of the industrial age,
Automobiles coming into being,
Would become a transportation rage.
It was a struggle for survival,
Between autos and horse drawn carriage,
And with no hope of coexistence,
Drove horse and buggy to disparage.

Few in the neighborhood owned an automobile,
Making a day at the beach out of reach,
The solution to this inconvenience was,
Getting six families at one dollar each.
Six dollars a truck load for hire would be,
On Harold Knight's large moving van,
We'd be transported to Apponaug shores,
To frolic at the beach in the sand.

Preparations would be made for this event,
With food, cool drinks and good cheer,
An abundance of towels and blankets,
And for grown-ups, a tub of iced beer.
All families, Costa, Pacheco, and White,
Added cousins, and all of us Rays,
Would meet new kids for the first time,
That made for an eventful day.

Boys would play with boys,
As girls were just a distraction,
But to me, I noticed shyly,
To a pretty little girl I was attracted.
Beyond that time, I have little recall,
How that day at the beach had ended,
And the thought of that pretty little girl,
From my mind I temporarily surrendered.

Now it was a summer past recollection,
And the meeting of families no more.
The automobiles were manufactured en masse,
When everyone could drive to the shore.
And along with the perfection of automobile,
They manufactured machinery of war,
What came to use would be a period of infamy,
Followed by peace and fighting no more.

Now I again chance to meet this young lady,
Who long ago shared a bit of my life,
That pretty little girl of Apponaug beach,
Who one day became my wife.
Yes, it was the 28th of June '47,

That Mary and I did wed,
I can't imagine what would become of me,
Had she married someone other instead.

Again, as we celebrate this Christmas season,
In the year of our Lord '93,
I say to Mary, my wife of forty-six years,
"Grow old with me, pretty lady,
The best is yet to be."

– *By your ever loving husband, George, December 25, 1993*

Footnote: *There remains a shared disagreement between Mary and me, regarding the identity of the pretty little girl at the beach as not being her. Mary says that it is a figment of my imagination. I say it is moot at this point in time. If it wasn't her in body, surely it was in spirit. As they say, "Fait accompli."*

HAPPY BIRTHDAY, MARY

Dear Mary:

For every year a candle glowed,
You have stood by me,
When we started out years ago,
In good times and adversities.

For every year a candle glowed,
On your birthday cake,
It sends a message loud and clear,
Your contribution a marriage makes.

Not only are you a loving wife,
You're also my dearest friend,
And no matter what the future brings,
I'll be with you 'til God says when.

Throughout our lives we've held together,
With ups and downs and no regrets,
But the greatest asset that's been accrued,
Being married to you, by far, the greatest yet.

So Happy Birthday, Mary.
– Your loving husband, George, August 23, 1995

CHRISTMAS ON GREENE STREET

We enjoyed many wonderful Christmases in the house on 50 Greene Street well provided for by my parents. Even though there were lean years in the lace trade when my father was "laid off" for lack of orders, I never felt that we had to go without at Christmas.

The exterior of the house was always tastefully decorated with candles in the windows and a door decoration of a large candy cane embellished with a spray of white pine handmade by my mother and lit by spotlights. There were no multi-colored chasing lights strung on the shrubbery. Mr. Dan McIver, the owner of Bradford Soap Works, who lived across the street complimented the effect commenting to my father, "Very nice. Simple, but effective!"

The interior decoration always included a large live tree that inevitably caused tension and general discord between my parents while getting it into the antiquated stand, into the house and standing up straight. Once the lights were strung and all lit, another challenge laced with muttered colorful language, I could help decorate. The ornaments were of the beautiful "Shiny Brite" frosted variety (vintage today) and the tinsel was made of actual aluminum strands which we layered on in abundance. Everything was carefully preserved and used again year after year.

My mother's pride was a nativity scene with twelve inch scale figures with a large stable that she treated like porcelain, although it was not. She originally spotted a Hummel set that she loved at Tally's Religious Articles Store but the price tag was far too dear. She chose instead a beautiful hand painted, fifteen piece set with Baby Jesus, Mary, Joseph, the three Magi, a drummer boy, two shepherds, assorted lambs, a cow, a donkey, a camel, and an angel to hang at the peak of the stable. My father fashioned a light on the inside of the stable to illuminate the Holy Family.

No one in my family set up an elaborate *"presépio"* with multiple levels of village scenes with the Holy Family as the focus surrounded by hundreds of pieces, as many Portuguese do. Whether due to lack of space or expendable funds, I never saw this type of large scale nativity display in my youth. I did not learn of this custom until I was in my fifties when I began to connect to my Portuguese heritage outside of my family in earnest.

Of course, the dining room table was beautifully set with candy and nuts, baked treats, homemade Portuguese liqueurs. My mother baked an amazing variety of specialty cookies and my *Vovó Maria Conceição*, her mother, made the best cake-like Portuguese sweet bread—a large *"bolo"* (loaf) for each family and a small one for each grandchild.

As a child, I always received something on Christmas morning that I really wanted in addition to things that I really needed, such as pajamas. My stocking always held goodies including a large bag of M&M's, a large candy cane shaped like a barber pole, and a naval orange in the toe. It was tradition.

Tradition. There are customs that families carry out the same way year after year after year, and ours was no exception. Working out whether the Rays or the Furtados would have our presence on Christmas Day brooked no argument. There was no question that it would be the Rays during Christmas afternoon much to my mother's discontent. Because we all lived in the same town in West Warwick, an oddity these days, there was pressure to be sure that everyone was visited.

So it went like this: On Christmas Eve, a thirty minute visit was expected with the Ray grandparents where the brothers, sister, and cousins came and went delivering presents. It was the Ray custom to open presents on Christmas Eve. Then to the Furtados for a more leisurely visit with the grandparents and perhaps a drink and a treat. Then back home and early to bed to be sure that Santa would come, unless I was much older when I was probably singing in the choir at midnight Mass.

On Christmas morning, it was elation at the crack of dawn to see what Santa had brought. As I was young then, it meant hurry up, get dressed in your new Christmas dress and winter coat and hat for the nine a.m. Mass as St. Anthony's Church. Back home for breakfast, because it was fasting since midnight before communion in those days, grab one toy, and then to the Ray grandparents' house for dinner at twelve noon.

What commotion! What bedlam! At our largest, there were twenty-one of us crammed into that little house. The men were bringing in saw horses and planks to set up the makeshift tables in the small kitchen; women were bringing in covered dishes and working in the tiny pantry with *Vovó* (grandmother); cousins were running everywhere showing off their new toys. My cousin Stephen brought a repeating toy gun one year that drove *Vovô* (our grandfather) to distraction. One year Aunt Evelyn made pudding and jello cups for dessert, but, on the way from their house, Uncle Ernie had to brake fast sliding the whole tray to the car floor. After dinner, the boys were caught jumping on the beds upstairs, so that was it, said *Vovô*: "Out!"

Now it was time for visiting "house-to-house." That means we visited all the homes of all the five siblings, but there was an order to it, a specific geographical sequence to follow. First, on the itinerary was Evelyn's because it was just around the corner on Clyde Street. One year, Santa brought them a new stereo system so we were greeted with the peels of Christmas chimes piped outside as we parked near the house. Only thirty minutes to see all their presents, grab a drink and a treat and off to... Frankie's house just down the hill. Thirty minutes there then across town to our house (George's) on Greene Street. My mother always dreaded those thirty minutes of cousins running amuck in her house and brothers drinking in the kitchen. (Things were getting pretty merry by then). Next up, Alfred's just up the street also on Greene Street, repeat. Lastly, we ended up at Tommy's, on Colvin Street at that time, where we could stay a little longer.

Not so fast! We still had to go to the Furtados where *Vovó Maria Conceição* had saved us some Christmas dinner so we could have supper with them and the Furtado uncles, aunts and cousins. We finally returned home by 8 or 9 p.m. that night...exhausted. If the weather was dry, it was easy enough to manage your footwear but if the weather was wet or snowy, it meant removing and donning your winter boots...seven times that day.

This was Christmas year after year until the grandparents began to pass away and the fabric of the family as we knew it began to unravel. Now each of the Ray siblings was the patriarch/matriarch of their own family as their children married and their grandchildren were born. Then the cycle began anew. Yet still, there was a security in that crazy, hectic tradition and it remains one of the fondest memories of my childhood. It was indeed a very merry Christmas and my father loved spending the day all together with his mother, father, siblings and their families.

By the time Dad had penned the following poem about Christmas, his parents had long passed. I have no doubt, however, that Christmas was one of his favorite times of year, in spite of his quarrels with the Christmas tree. It was not only because he had happy childhood memories of Christmas, as poor as they were, but because holidays spent while serving abroad in the Army made him appreciate them all the more.

THE INNOCENCE OF CHILDREN

The innocence of children,
Imbued with unsullied love,
Like sprinkled heavenly stardust,
Dispensed by angels from above.

Cleanliness is next to Godliness,
And innocence akin as well,
Though ignorance sometimes called bliss,
In hearts of many dwell.

Viewed in childhood's mirthful glee,
Mirrors joy in children's minds,
May we all behave as they,
At this joyous Christmas time.

As an infant, the Christ Child knew,
His arrival may confusion cause,
So to share His joy with others,
He created SANTA CLAUS!

– *Joseph "George" Ray, Written with Season's Greetings, Christmas, 1995*

This was shared with the residents of the Villa of St. Antoine as a Christmas card from George in December, 2005.

DABBLING FOR MARIE

While Dad's interest in writing came later in life, it seems that he showed a talent for drawing at a much earlier age. While I was a child, Dad would pick up a pencil from time to time and try his hand at a sketch. This might have been encouraged by my interest in a television program in the 1950s called "Learn to Draw With Jon Gnagy." It was a syndicated series of fifteen minute drawing lessons that ran from 1950 to 1955 and was considered a children's show. Each lesson would work on a technique such as shading or perspective culminating in a finished pencil and charcoal sketch.

This TV show gave rise to a product called "The Jon Gnagy Learn to Draw Outfit" which I asked for and received for Christmas one year. It had everything you needed to produce basic still life and landscape drawings with pencils and charcoals following a step-by-step instruction booklet. I studied and practiced with it sometimes asking Dad for help. He understood what to do with it right away and, on occasion, would try his hand at a sketch. He sketched me in profile, banana curls and all, on a whim, when I was about eight years of age using that kit. This sketch still survives sixty-five years later.

Dad also tried painting with oil but never invested in the supplies or the equipment. Instead he tacked a piece of oilcloth to a pegboard near his workbench in the basement and used leftover odd oil paint samples to work on a nativity scene copied from a Christmas card. He would work on it from time to time but never finished it.

What Dad did complete, however, was a painting in oil that he copied from an ad for Carter's baby clothes. He drew the chubby baby with an angelic smile wearing his father's hat and gloves freehand on oilcloth and painted it with his odds 'n ends oil paints. It was framed in wood from leftover pieces of crown molding that he made himself. That piece hung over my bed well into my teen years never making me feel that it was too childish. The point is that while he never had the time nor inclination to spend money on supplies for such a hobby, what few works that Dad tried his hand at, he made for me.

DATING AND SAILORS

As the only child of a protective Portuguese father, I held little hope of ever having a social life that involved dating boys before I reached the age of eighteen. Negotiating when I would be allowed to date came to a head in our home when I was fifteen and a sophomore in high school. Thanks to my mother's intervention, I was allowed to accept an invitation by an upperclassman to the Senior Informal Dance that fall. Dad was none too pleased at the idea of his innocent fifteen year old daughter going out in a "car date" with a Senior boy. I overheard him arguing with my mother that letting me go out alone in a car with a boy of seventeen who was already shaving was "out of the question." At the time, I did not understand what shaving had to do with anything. After all it was only a school dance and my curfew was 10:00 p.m. with no going out later. We had a nice enough time but that boy didn't ask me out again.

Somehow I managed to have other dates and a steady boyfriend throughout high school until I left for college. After that my choices were my own although always cautioned to have *"Juízo na cabeça!"*–the Portuguese admonition to "Use your head and don't do anything stupid!"

Between Thanksgiving and Christmas of my sophomore year at the University of Rhode Island, my sorority organized a bus to transport us to the Navy USO in Newport for a mixer with the sailors. It seemed like a patriotic thing to do around the holidays for servicemen away from home during this Viet Nam era. I thought my father would approve, if he knew about it, although I did not need his permission. I met a sweet guy named Mike from Philadelphia who asked for my phone number. I gave it but said I'd be home for Christmas break and he should call me there.

Accustomed to calling my own shots by now, I invited Mike home to 50 Greene Street without asking permission or even giving it a thought that I should. Dad saw red! "What? You invited a sailor that you picked up at a USO mixer to this house?" he cried. "He could come in here, stick a knife in my gut, and rob us blind!" Remember, Dad had been in the Army and he must have witnessed rough encounters between soldiers and sailors on liberty during his time in the service. He clearly did not have a high opinion of sailors.

The short of the story is that Mike had taken a bus from Newport to Providence and hitchhiked to West Warwick on a cold, windy December day arriving at our front door shivering and frozen to the bone. Dad's heart melted to see this poor kid, and not a burly 300 pound Bluto, standing there. His memory went back to World War II and what it was like to be a kid away from home during the holidays. Of course, Dad invited him in, fed him, and chatted him up like he was his son. By the time I returned to college after Christmas break, I decided not to see Mike again. Dad asked about him though: "What happened to Mike? He was a nice guy!"

It wasn't long after that on a Friday the 13th in February 1970 that I met David Fraley through a sorority sister at the Blue Door (a popular dance and booze joint) in

Narragansett. Dave was a parachute rigger in the Navy stationed at Quonset Point on sea duty. It was the typical Rhode Island girl meets Navy guy story. We dated that spring before he was due to ship out in May for a North Atlantic cruise for four months. This looked serious because he asked me to keep his car for him for the summer while he was at sea, so I brought Dave, *another sailor*, home to meet Mom and Dad before he shipped out. Not as worried about my judgment at this point, Dad took an instant liking to Dave. We married on June 9, 1973 and settled in southern New England moving a couple of times between Rhode Island and nearby Massachusetts. Mom and Dad treated Dave like the son they never had as long as they lived.

The feeling was mutual on Dave's part and he still continues to hold affection and warm memories of his father-in-law even to this day:

> *"I don't say it lightly. My father-in-law was more than a father figure to me. When you are young and have been far away from home for a long time, you miss the connection of a mature male in your life. I don't know if I ever told him how much he meant to me, but relied on that 'guy thing' that magically transfers unsaid feelings to other people without having to move your lips.*
>
> *"George Ray was a man I admired from the first day I met him. He made me feel welcome with a warmth that was genuine and unconditional. If I did things that made him crazy or disappointed, I never felt it in his demeanor."*

Over the years, Dave has stored many special memories of his father-in-law as their relationship grew and deepened. He has contributed some of the most endearing.

> *"Many things stand out, but a few moments are worth sharing:*
>
> *"Marie and I were setting up a 'new' apartment and it did not come with a refrigerator. Short on funds, we went to a second or third hand store to buy one for $100. We asked George to help us move it with the shop truck. When we arrived, and he sees the size of the white whale, he tells the owner of the store to plug it in to make sure it works. The owner refuses stating that he knows it works otherwise he wouldn't sell it (with attitude). George says, 'If I move this*

all the way to Massachusetts and it doesn't work, I'm bringing it back and it's going to come right through your window!' George Ray was very protective of us!

"We had gone for a ride with my in-laws and were exiting the interstate in the middle of an unexpected snow storm. I hit the brakes and we start to slide down the ramp and it appeared that we were going to slide into cars that had stopped at the light at the bottom of the ramp. George jumps out of the car as it is sliding down the incline and starts pushing on the front fender in an effort to direct it away from the stationary cars. It worked!

"On a sightseeing trip to Boston, we were wandering around Faneuil Hall shopping area and George says to me, 'Go over there and get us four hot dogs and four drinks. Here's a twenty.' I get back with the food and after a long pause he says, 'Where's my change?' I said, 'George, there was no change.' You could see the child of the Depression in his face as he struggled to understand how four hot dogs and four drinks could cost more than $20. I don't think he enjoyed lunch that day.

"I had a business associate that had two extra tickets to a luxury box at Fenway Park for a Red Sox game, so I asked George if he wanted to go. He said he did. He loved having unlimited hot dogs and hamburgers and cold drinks and a private bathroom and a seat that no one could kick behind him. He was beaming during and after the game. Several weeks later I had access to tickets and asked him if he wanted to go. 'Luxury box?' he asked. 'No,' I said, 'but right on the field near first base.' He replied quickly, 'No, thanks. Why don't you take someone else?' Clearly, I had spoiled him for any other Fenway experience."

– David Fraley

When Dad began writing in the 1990s, he took to including poems in our birthday and Christmas cards. The following is one that he wrote for Dave on the occasion of his forty-sixth birthday:

BIRTHDAY WISHES

Contestants came to join the fray,
To greet the challenge from first day born,
All numbered, poised at the starting line,
In a lifelong race called a marathon.

Some bolted out in a hurried start,
To impress viewers along the line,
Without a plan of strength conserved,
Soon faltered and fell far behind.

But those who paced and planned with skill,
Continued despite hardships faced,
Accepted pain with grace and pride,
Continued forward in measured pace.

So on this birthday of a milestone set,
Has run a good race from first day born,
And keep in mind, yet Heartbreak Hill,
To run this race called a marathon.

HAPPY BIRTHDAY, DAVE!

OUR LOVE IS LIKE A MARATHON.
YOUR RACE IS OUR RACE, AND WILL ALWAYS BE.

– George and "Mother-in-Law," March 15, 1995

GRANDSONS

An old Jewish lady was once heard to say, "Children are the investment, but grandchildren are the dividends." Having invested all their love, energy, and resources in one child, George and Mary Ray were certainly anxious to reap the dividends. Married in our early twenties with careers to build, Dave and I were not in a hurry to start a family. Finally ready six years later we were able to make the announcement on my mother's birthday by presenting her with a birthday card that read "Happy Birthday, Grandma!" Sharing the news that we were expecting the following April was our birthday surprise to her. The elation was off the charts!

The birth of John McComas Fraley, II, named for his paternal grandfather, in April of 1980 was a blessed event. The much awaited and anticipated first grandchild of Truth and Mack Fraley as well as that of George and Mary Ray certainly placed him in a special position.

Four years later, our second son, Benjamin Gibson Fraley, arrived in June of 1984, doubling our blessings and our joy. The two boys mirrored the family dynamics of Truth and Mack Fraley who had also raised two sons, but for George and Mary who had limited their family to an only daughter, it was a different situation. George and Mary frequently babysat the boys while I worked parttime and it took all their energy to keep up with them, together as a bundle of perpetual motion and separately, each with his own interests and needs. Nevertheless, as different as the boys were, they were both cherished for their unique personalities and gifts.

About the time that John was eight years of age and Ben was four, Mom and Dad thought it would be great fun to set up an Easter egg hunt in their yard on Easter Sunday. Mom got busy filling plastic eggs with candy and trinkets but it was Dad's idea to add quarters.

On Easter Sunday of 1988, shortly after arriving at 50 Greene Street, the challenge was put forth to the boys. Each supplied with a straw basket with their name tag attached, they were set off in the backyard and the chase was on! John, being substantially older and understanding the goal, was off gathering eggs with no problem leaving his poor little brother in the dust. As soon as Grandma realized that John was finding all the eggs and that Ben had none, she immediately called a halt to the contest, reorganized the rules, and made them start over. For every brightly colored egg that John found, Ben had to have a turn to find one next so that each would have an equal number of eggs in his basket at the end.

In the years that followed, each boy had his name on an egg so they could only pick up his own egg and leave the other. Dad, wanting to make it more challenging, drew up a map similar to pirates seeking buried treasure that John took charge of but was charged with helping Ben along the process. Grandma was satisfied that each boy was treated fairly and equally and Dad was happy that he devised a way for the older to help the younger and thereby collaborate.

That map was saved and used year after year with the dates noted of each subsequent Easter Egg Hunt until they became too old for it. The map is a bit tattered and frayed and the colorful drawings of Dad's artwork have faded but it is a cherished souvenir of a happy holiday and the care and affection that *Vovô* and Grandma showed for their *netinhos* (grandsons) in making holidays special.

Among many of the notes and poems that were tucked in the boys' cards by their *Vovô*, the Portuguese endearment for Grandpa, the following is addressed to John during Christmas of 1994 when he was fourteen years of age.

A TIME FOR REFLECTION

"*Dear John,*

It's been known that the first born has the advantages of attention and, because of his needs as an infant, the world is his to enjoy. That is, until the second born arrives. That being the case with Ben, who required similar attention, may have created in you feelings of being cast aside for the want of attention for Ben. I believe you know now as a young man that is the furthest from the truth. I also feel you understand that Ben looks up to you as his big brother and loves you very much. Much like your Uncle Steve looked up to your Dad in similar times. Having said that in writing, I've enclosed a little poem which I believe speaks of how we feel about you as a loving person and a loving grandson.

Sometime in the middle of October,
An announcement was made to me,
That the coming of a newborn,
Would be added to a family of three.
So, in the month of June '84,
A bundle of joy would become,
The fourth member of the family Fraley,
On the 8th, an angel delivered a son.

His given name would be Benjamin,
In Hebrew means favored one,
And John, also in Hebrew,
Is called the gracious one.
For of neither the favored nor gracious,
No one is loved more nor shunned,
In the eyes and hearts of we who love,
BOTH ARE LOVED AS ONE.

MERRY CHRISTMAS
From GRANDMA AND VOVÔ, *December, 1994"*

Now an adult, his grandson, John, has developed a mature perspective of all that his grandfather was trying to convey to him. One never knows which of our words or actions will impact the life of a child. Dad would be surprised and touched, I think, to read John's thoughts and memories.

"*My Vovô was a man who was given little, but gave much, and the way he did everything was as important as anything.*

"*Without the benefit of a formal education or inherited money, he made himself into someone who could pass on knowledge and wealth to the most important people in his life: his family. George Ray was so able because of his inquisitive mind, work* ethic, and willingness to sacrifice comfort now for investment in tomorrow. The self-respect these qualities gave him never strayed into pride and therefore he was never afraid to try something new. Even if the first attempt wasn't ideal, Vovô would always try again and again with better results each time. Others might be intimidated by a lack of pedigree or resources or any other excuse, but not George Ray. While his proudest achievements were the daughter he raised, the business he built, and these writings that you hold in your hands, one of his hobbies might best reveal his character: wood working.

"My prized possession is a carved, wooden horse that he made. It looks like a wild leader of a herd, chestnut brown with white highlights, and it exudes the power and majesty of the animal. George Ray was able to capture, without formal training, the essence of this creature as a sculptor would, with correct anatomical proportions, a pose that suggests movement and a dynamic design that hints at a story. All this made with simple tools and materials, but born from his drive to give something of himself to his grandson and his inability to remain idle in his golden years (these writings are even further testament to that tendency!). I loved it from the moment he gave it to me as a teenager, but I have to confess that wasn't always the case.

"The first horse he gave me was a smaller gray work horse that looked more like the block of wood it was carved from than anything equine. I remember thinking it was dull, crude and I couldn't understand why I was getting it. I didn't know why he felt the need to make it, why I would want it or what went into its creation. My lack of enthusiasm did not deter him, of course. As he built more and more, one could see his technique and eye quickly improve and by the time he made the brown horse he had accomplished what he set out to do. You could see the willingness to work, iterate and improve in the wood itself. I try to keep this lesson with me whenever I am discouraged or afraid of failure and I am reminded of it when I look at this carving. For the qualities that led Vovô to carve wood underpinned everything he did in life.

"These words you hold in your hands were also the product of a craftsman refining his skills. Perhaps he would never reach the level of a master with all the advantages and talent one could have, but that didn't matter. George Ray set himself to express himself in the world in whatever media he chose, despite starting from scratch. The character to undertake the creative process, whether in wood or in words, is as important as the output and reveals much about the creator.

"Parkinson's Disease would eventually rob him of his ability to express himself in so many ways, but we could always tell that the need to create and communicate his feelings could not be stolen. He would save up his words and energy to deliver a well-timed joke or piece of wisdom, though these occasions would be fewer and fewer as time went on. Near the end, when he knew there wouldn't be many more occasions to do so, he gathered my brother and I to pass on what he had learned over his years. Those lessons were another gift for my brother and I, honed over a lifetime, and are ours to keep. But like this book and his carved horses and everything else that George Ray set himself to, the bravery he exhibited in expressing himself, despite challenges at the beginning and end of his life, speaks volumes."
– John Fraley

The carved horse handmade by George Ray for his grandson, John, inscribed underneath "J.G.Ray #6, March, 1990."

FOR BENJAMIN

We celebrate on the 8th of June,
'Cause he's one year plus ten,
With eleven candles on his birthday cake,
We send our best wishes to Ben.

To us he's number #1 in hockey,
'Cause he's fearless as can be,
When pucks come flying towards his net,
No shot will enter free.

He's also good in baseball,
For he's a sport and knows the score,
But most of all he's our Grandson,
That's reason enough to love him more.

Happy Birthday, Ben!
You will forever be loved.

– Grandma and Vovô, June 8, 1995

Obviously, Dad never hesitated to take advantage of what is now called a "teachable moment" with his grandsons. One of Benjamin's most vivid memories of such an object lesson comes from when he was very young on one of their many after school outings:

"I don't think I was older than four years old. Vovô had picked me up from pre-school at Mercymount Country Day. As was our custom, Vovô was driving me to either McDonald's for lunch or the nearby General Store to pick up my favorite snack. This was a normal post-school activity that I was able to convince Vovô was a good idea. I would get in Vovô's car and request immediately that we go. Vovô's response was usually, "But I don't know where to go." "That's ok, Vovô. I'll tell you where to go."

As we were driving, Vovô shared some sage advice with me.

He said, "Ben, do you see the speed limit sign?"

I said, "Yes."

He then asked, "Do you see how fast it says the car is going?"

I said, "Yes."

"They are the same, right?" He asked.

"Yup."

"That's called following the law."

Vovô was always a consistent example of discipline, correctness, and hard work. When I think about this memory, it reminds me of Vovô's sometimes comical character. In retrospect, I believe that he was a teacher in his own right. Vovô felt it was important that he pass on his experiences and character in small lessons, anecdotes, and advice. Most of us don't remember everything we were ever taught, but those object lessons stay with us."

— Benjamin Fraley

AND FOR ME...

FOR MY DAUGHTER ON HER 47TH BIRTHDAY

Thank you for being a good daughter,
For understanding our conservative quirks,
And for all the times we had to skimp,
When Daddy was out of work.

Thank you for your forgiveness,
For accepting No! as a rule so extreme,
How you must have felt we were unfair,
And thought of us as plain old mean.

Now that you're older and wiser,
And know times are not always turtledove
It's what we did, as you do now,
In these days called tough love.

So on the threshold of truth and wisdom,
Knowing life's neither sunny nor gray,
Set your compass towards positive thinking,
AND HAVE THE HAPPIEST OF ALL BIRTHDAYS!

Dad and Mom, September 3, 1997

AND A LITTLE DITTY DAD SANG TO ME AS A CHILD

CELEBRATION IN DIVERSITY

I remember when...

"Come to my party today if you please,
Roses and lilies will dance in the breeze.
There will be people there you will see,
Frenchmen, Italians, and Port-u-guese.
And, a few Jewish, Irish, and Polish kids, too!"

June 9, 1970 at Old St. Paul's Church, Wickford, RI. Dad ready to walk me down the aisle on my wedding day.

IN-LAWS

By my marriage to David Fraley, our small family was extended to southwest Virginia to include Truth and Mack Fraley. They were lovely people with whom we all enjoyed a very warm and close relationship. In the in-law department, I felt that I was very lucky especially in regard to my mother-in-law, Truth, who was a wonderful friend and confidante.

George and Truth struck up an excellent rapport, so that when Truth was diagnosed with breast cancer in 1994, Dad was as crushed as we all were. In the fall of 1994, Dad began to write letters of encouragement and support to Truth often including many of his most humorous and uplifting pieces. An excerpt from one such letter follows:

"November 7, 1994

Dear Truth,

I find myself in thoughts about you as a person and why you are up front in a line of people I so admire. Not only because you are the mother of Dave whom I love as my own son, but largely because of the fitting name that you were given at birth—Truth. What a beautiful name for a beautiful person. Truth, I do so love you as a friend and as family, and to quote one of my favorites, 'I love those who love the ones I love.'

I hope you're feeling better. If not, you will be because so many prayers are being sent to Mary, the Blessed Mother of Jesus for your recovery...

Your friend, George"

Truth passed away from the dreaded cancer shortly thereafter on February 21, 1995. She was a teacher, counselor, and spirited adventurer always willing to try new things. Later in life, she tried her hand at crewel embroidery creating some beautifully intricate needlework pieces that are still cherished and hang in our home. For George and Mary Ray, she stitched a large framed wall hanging of red poppies that hung in their dining room at 50 Greene Street. After Truth's passing, Dad wrote the following in memorial to her.

A TAPESTRY OF RED FLOWERS

A tapestry of framed red flowers,
Adorns our household wall,
It hangs as a sentinel in tribute,
Of one's life, one's all.

A tapestry of framed red flowers,
Speaks reticent but clear,
Though in journey far away,
Dear Truth is forever near.

A tapestry of framed red flowers,
Created gift, toiled by nimble hands,
It manifests cherished memories,
Glass encased, edged in gold leaf strands.

A tapestry of framed red flowers,
In concert all in hymn we sing,
Enter, Truth Smith Fraley, through heaven's gates,
Opened wide, on angel's wings.

In Memorial: Truth Smith Fraley, (1925–1995)
– Joseph "George" Ray, April 22, 1995

Part Four:
The Lace Trade

While many are aware of the thriving textile industry that attracted European immigrants to New England at the turn of the twentieth century, few know about the lace manufacturing trade that was the mainstay of the livelihoods of the Ray brothers. All four brothers, Frankie, Alfred, George, and Tommy together represented 160 years working as lace weavers, or "twisthands," as it was known, but none of them in as diverse roles as my father, George.

Dad liked to say that lace was always a part of his life from childhood to retirement. From a baby crawling on the webs that were brought home for "pulling lace" at night, to twenty years of working a Leavers lace machine, to his union activities, to ten years in management in quality control, to ten years of co-ownership in a lace company, lace was the warp thread of his life, and consequently ours as a family.

LEAVERS LACE

A little known segment of the textile industry in Rhode Island is the manufacture of what is known as Leavers lace. The making of lace may conjure images of ladies sitting around tatting or weaving lace by hand, which is known as "needle, bobbin, or pillow lace."[xxvii] Handmade lace was a painstaking and lengthy process that made lace a very expensive and rare commodity over the centuries until the establishment of lace production by machine. John Levers adapted Heathcoat's Old Loughborough machine while working in a garret on Derby Road in Nottingham, England in 1813. The original machine made net, that was needed for mosquito netting by the military, but it was found that the Jacquard apparatus for creating patterned lace could be adapted to it.

Modern Leaver (the "a" was added to Levers' name) lace machines are massive weighing about 17 tons, having 40,000 moving parts, and carrying between 12,000 and 50,000 threads.[xxviii] A black powdered graphite was used as a lubricant in the manufacture of Leaver lace on those parts of the machine which carry the bobbins and bobbin plates.[xxix] The black lead-based graphite would render the lace product soiled and the lace weaver himself covered with the substance on his work clothes, on his skin, and embedded under his fingernails. The wives of lace weavers dismayed at the filthy clothes that the workers wore home. My mother, for one, required my father to strip to his underwear in the basement so that the work clothes could go right into the laundry soaking tub before he bathed. Nevertheless, dirty work clothes meant there was work to be had and therefore, a paycheck.

In terms of the process of lacemaking, designs are first drawn on paper by a drafter and then "translated" onto punch cards (much like old computer keypunch cards) and fed into the Jacquard machine that reads the pattern. Winders place each thread onto bobbins which are placed into carriages that are inserted into the machine. The lace weaver has the responsibility for setting up the carriages and "tying in" threads ensuring that every thread is in exactly the right position. The weaver must also be able to adjust the weights, balance, tension, and timing to ensure that the pattern is rendering properly. Unlike lace production that embroiders a pattern onto a piece of fabric, Leavers lace is woven with a particular characteristic "twist" that makes the result not only beautifully intricate but strong enough not to unravel when cut. Hence, lace weavers are also known as "twisthands."

I still remember Dad bringing me to the mill at Valley Lace Company when I was a little girl. The noise of all those machines running was deafening! I can still see to this day the image of the lace pattern coming up on the machine. It was so clear and detailed that I remarked, "Daddy, I didn't know you made wallpaper here!" It looked to me like the striped and floral wallpaper in my grandmother's front parlor.

Once the weaving process itself is completed, the web is removed from the machine and sent to inspectors and menders to repair any holes or defects. Then the web in its "greige"[xxx] form goes to the dye house where it is bleached to remove any traces of the graphite lubricant and dyed to the color specification.[xxxi] A mill's complex could include several sections, such as the weaving shed, mending room, the dye house, and a boiler house in addition to administrative offices.

It is clear to see that the Leavers lace that made up a table cloth, a dress, or the band trim on lingerie, blouses, ladies handkerchiefs or sheets and pillowcases, was a multi-faceted process that involved highly trained and skilled lace weavers as well as many auxiliary workers. Below is a photo from June 18, 1935 of the Valley Lace Company[xxxii] staff where the Ray brothers devoted most of their working lives. Dad's brother Frankie at age 17, shown below the white arrow, worked at Valley Lace Company as a warper, beamer, and later as a lace weaver. This photo, courtesy of brother Frankie (Francis Ray) was featured in an Amby Smith article about the lace trade in Rhode Island in the *Kent County Daily Times*, July 30, 1996 for which Dad provided the source material.

Remembering the many artisans who helped create prosperity in the Valley

Requirements for training and employment as a lace weaver were stringent and controlled by the trade union. According to the Amalgamated Lace Operatives of America, Leaver Section, a candidate for the position of weaver was required to begin as a "floor boy" for six months before qualifying to begin as an apprentice.[xxxiii] An apprentice was defined as "any male person between the ages of 20 and 30 years, who has operated a lace machine for less than three years."[xxxiv] Moreover, it was the Shop Committee with Management who were "responsible in placing apprentices on machines with teachers who, in their opinion, will carry out the responsibility of properly teaching the apprentice in the operation of a lace machine."[xxxv]

It was not an easy trade to break into. Quotas of accepted apprentices were proportioned per journeyman lacemaker and strictly controlled by the trade union. Because of the origination of Leaver lace manufacturing in England, it followed that it was the English in America who were responsible for establishing the businesses and importing the machines and therefore, hired immigrants from England who were skilled in assembling, maintaining, and running the machines. In fact, the Portuguese were specifically excluded for some time because they were considered "not smart enough" as told by Dad's Uncle Joe Furtado (Pacheco). He was the first Portuguese man to qualify and work as a lace weaver in the Pawtuxet Valley. Having broken that glass ceiling, all four of his Ray nephews followed along the trail that he blazed.

This is not to say that the Portuguese were not hired by the lace manufacturers in other areas of the thirty-two processes involved in producing the final product. Lacemaking requires a great deal of auxiliary help and the Portuguese filled those positions as threaders and menders (women's jobs), as beamers or warpers or in the dye house doing the bleaching and dying. However, there were only about six or seven Portuguese lace weavers in all of Rhode Island's forty-two mills according to best recollection.[xxxvi]

PULLING LACE

During the Great Depression, one way that Portuguese immigrant families in the valley augmented their income was by "pulling lace" in the evenings after the day's work and the usual chores were done. The task was to pull out the running threads of the large piece or "web" of lace to separate the bands of lace and then wind the bands onto cards earning pennies per card. Band lace was typically used to trim lingerie and linens, as opposed to "all over" large pieces used for dressmaking and tablecloths.

Dad recalled vividly that, as young as the age of seven, it was his job after attending Highland Street School to collect a "web" of band lace from the Lippitt mill at the bottom of the hill of Wakefield Street so that the family could work on it during the evening after supper. Everyone, even the children, were expected to pitch in and help. The next morning at the crack of dawn, George loaded the finished work into a wagon, proceeded down the hill, picking up his cousin Dorothy on the way, to deliver the load at the mill before school. That afternoon after school he would stop at the mill again to pick up another load and the process would repeat itself.

My mother also remembered well the late hours of pulling lace in the evenings at home but recalls that her brothers often found something better to do leaving her and her mother to do it. Dad refers to this time in his poem, "Little People of the Thirties" that seems to evoke a sad nostalgia for the responsibilities expected of children at such a young age during those times of hardship.

LITTLE PEOPLE OF THE THIRTIES

Through the prism of the Great Depression,
It's a premise widely known,
That children of the thirties,
Lacked pleasures currently found.
In mining towns where the Mason-Dixon meets
And in other places with labor needs,
Children worked in coal mines,
Shuffling screened coal with their feet.

Here in the northeast,
Where conditions were equally compared,
There were many towns throughout,
Where the poor had little to share.
However of one redeeming salvation,
Arose a cottage trade as it was known,
Of the "pulling" and carding of lace,
In the privacy of one's own home.

We children were given a share,
Of lace bands we were obliged to pull,
And many times staying up late,
So tired, fell asleep at school,
The bands were some thirty-six yards in length,
And paid a penny each or more,
To separate, card and bundle,
And return to the company store.

Poor Mama carried the heaviest burden,
While maintaining a home so neat,
Many nights staying up much later,
For an order's schedule to meet.
In the morning, we were rousted from bed,
To deliver the lace to the mill
We would moan at the very thought,
Of facing that early dawn chill.

The distance of travel to deliver,
Was three miles or more to the mill,
To see two youngsters shuffling,
With a wagon-load of lace down the hill.
Where, at any time in the present,
Do children show such stoic diligence?
Could it have been a lesson learned,
From expected parental discipline?

Now as I near declining years,
My reflections strain to recall,
What manner of instinct possessed us,
Or were we not children at all?
Was it just a necessity of the times,

In society what was then the norm?
We were called "Children of the Thirties,"
Or, little people, too soon to be born.

– Joseph "George" Ray, December, 1993

LACE INDUSTRY BOOM AND BUST

The machine production of lace grew rapidly in the United States after World War II. Previously the birthplace of Leavers lace machines, the wartime destruction in England caused by the bombings created an opportunity for lace manufacture to take hold in the United States. The industry especially boomed when changes in the tariff laws made it profitable to import the lace-making machinery with Rhode Island soon becoming one of the important centers of lace manufacture in the United States.

In an interview with Amby Smith, Senior Scene Editor for the *Pawtuxet Valley Daily Times*, published July 30, 1996, Dad shared the 1965 Directory of the American Lace Manufacturing Industry. It listed 434 lace machines operating in Rhode Island far outstripping New Jersey (71), Connecticut (60), New York (53), Tennessee (32), and North Carolina (10) combined.

Dad's job as a lace weaver paid him well... when he was working. Our economic prosperity as a family rose or fell depending on the fashion of the day.

The Lace Mills in Rhode Island: 1965
Total: 42, Total Leaver Lace Machines: 434

Coventry	Greene Lace Works	Northeastern Lace	**North Scituate**
Abbott Laces, Inc.	George Hall Laces	Ronnie Lace	Sargent Lace Works
Berion Lace Works, Inc.	Hazel Laces	Royal Lace	**West Greenwich**
Beverly Lace Works, Inc.	Hilltop Lace	Steger Lace	Mishnock Lace
Bilmont Lace, Inc.	Havens Lace	Stella Lace	Wildwood Lace
Boeglin Lace	Kent Lace	Tiogue Lace	**West Warwick**
R. W. Clark Laces	Koszela Lace	Valley Lace	Harris Lace Works
Cousins	Kowal Lace	Washington Lace	Lubeth Lace
Crown Laces, Inc.	L. & L. Lace	**Hope**	Riverpoint Lace
Davie Lace, Inc.	L. & M. Lace	Bodell Lace	Winsor Lace
Fashion Lace	Linwood Lace	**Hope Valley**	Yena Lace
Gaspee Lace Works	Maguire Lace	Jim Beattie's Daughters Lace	York Lace

Source: "Remembering the many artisans who helped create prosperity in the Valley," Joseph G. Ray as told to Amby Smith, Pawtuxet Valley Times, July 30, 1966.

Growing Up Portuguese in the Lace Trade of the Pawtuxet Valley, Marie R. Fraley, April 23, 2018

If frilly lace blouses were in style, orders for lace were abundant from the clothing manufacturers and that meant Dad and all the lace weavers had work.

Royal weddings played a part as well. The bridal dress of the American actress, Grace Kelly, worn during her wedding to Prince Rainier III of Monaco on April 19, 1956 is cited as one of the most elegant and best-remembered bridal gowns of all time. Grace Kelly's wedding attire was estimated to have required 300 yards of the finest lace with an exquisite lace veil which featured an estimated 1,000 pearls. American brides rushed to find gowns styled like the one worn by the new Princess of Monaco spurring on orders for lace production to fill the demand.

Jackie Kennedy, wife of President John F. Kennedy, was known for her sleek Oleg Cassini fashions but her lace mantillas worn as a head covering to Mass between 1960 and 1963 had all of us wearing them as well. But then the Beatles hit American shores so the fashion abruptly changed to miniskirts, vinyl, and the very "mod" Mary Quant British styles by the mid-1960s. Lace was out and that meant that times were lean.

If the clothes manufacturers were not using lace, then the orders were not coming in from the Wiener Laces, Inc. head office in New York City and the weavers didn't work. That meant being "laid off;" not out of a job but without a paycheck because that depended upon hours worked. Dad was out of work for thirteen weeks one summer and even contemplated selling the house. I remember sitting beside him on the front porch steps of the house for which he worked so hard, seeing the worry on his face.

Fortunately, my mother was a child of the Depression and was used to economizing to the last penny. She shopped the sales, made my clothes, mended everything she could, and did without herself but we were okay, never missing a mortgage payment of $37.75 per month, because she was used to being careful. It was their habit to save any surplus cash even when times were good. What my father could never figure out was why others were being called back and were working, while he and his brothers, the Portuguese, were still waiting for the call for work. Make what you will of that, but I know it bothered him.

Besides "laid off," there were two other phrases heard in the household that signaled lean times. One was "changing patterns." The weavers were paid by the measure of a "rack" of lace produced, therefore, if there was a large order on a particular pattern then the machine ran and ran without interruption. Lots of racks were produced and good money was made during an eight hour shift. Then your "buddy," your work partner, would take over for the next eight hour shift and production continued. However, if you were tying in a new warp or had to change patterns, then your machine was not producing while you were "tying in" and did not get paid as much for down time.

The other very bad word we never wanted to hear when Dad came through the door was "Smash!" I'm not sure to this day exactly what that meant but, even as a child, I could tell by the look on his face and the tone of his voice that something had gone very wrong on the machine and there was a mess to be fixed. Obviously that also meant a lot of down time and no production.

UNION MAN

To be a lace weaver, at least in the northern states, one was required to be a dues paying member of the union, the Amalgamated Lace Operatives of America. Dad was a member of Leavers Branch #7 (one out of eleven Leavers branches), and for a time in the mid-1960s, was Corresponding Secretary of that branch. He would take care of any necessary written correspondence and pen notes from their branch for the newsletter, "The American Lace Worker." At that point in time, he was not very confident in his writing, so would turn to me for help. As I was still in high school and not a very good writer myself, we muddled through together, poring over the dictionary and the thesaurus looking for just the right words. Sometimes we overdid it with fifty-cent selections and convoluted sentences, but we were learning together.

Dad was involved in several initiatives, one of which included the establishment of a union pension fund for retired workers. It was never going to be enough to support a worker in their retirement but it would be supplementary to a worker's nest egg from contributions made over time. Unfortunately, the demise of the lace business and lack of workers to contribute to the fund did not allow the plan to fulfill its potential.

By this point in time, with the change in fashion to sleek and modern styles, it seemed that the handwriting was on the wall for the lace industry in the north. There were rumblings of moving lace mills to the southern states, such as Tennessee, North Carolina, and South Carolina, where energy and fuel as well as labor costs (without union interference) were cheaper.

In response to this, Dad became involved in an idea to help promote the lace industry in Rhode Island. It was called Project Leavers Lace, a public relations initiative to highlight the beauty and the quality of Leavers Lace. The centerpiece of the project was a dinner dance and fashion show, featuring lace fashions, at the Rhodes On the Pawtuxet ballroom in Cranston, Rhode Island. It was a grand event that took up much of Dad's spare time and energy as a member of that committee. It was a great success and ran for two years, but it did not "move the needle" much in terms of boosting orders.

One accomplishment, however, of which Dad was particularly proud was obtaining the attention and support of Governor John H. Chaffee in proclaiming May 1-6, 1966, Rhode Island Leavers Lace Week at ceremonies in the Governor's Office at the Rhode Island State House.

(L-R) Joseph G. Ray, public relations director of Project Leavers Lace; Gilbert "Ronnie" Bodell, Leavers Lace Manufacturers of America, Inc., Oliver Breton, director of Project Leavers Lace; RI Governor John H Chaffee; Robert Saywell, president of Leavers Lace Manufacturers of America, Inc., Frederick H Derham, secretary of Project Leavers Lace.

PROMOTION TO MANAGEMENT

Anything that Dad did, he did well. He had an insatiable curiosity about how things worked, so consequently, he was fully engaged in solving the problem at hand when they didn't. Dad not only expected the best of himself, but he expected the same of me. He'd say, "I'm number one in the mill, so you be number one in school." I never felt that it was a threat, only encouragement. As a matter of fact, it seemed that we were forging a partnership, a pact, that we would do whatever was in front of us to the best of our ability, no matter the outcome. There is no doubt that he set the bar high. He was quick with his praise for me and never showed disappointment when I missed the mark, as long as I did my best. Dad was always much harder on himself.

He approached his job as a lace weaver with that same level of conscientious commitment. Over the years, he earned the reputation of not only doing his job of weaving lace to near perfection but of understanding all facets of lace production. After so many years working at Valley Lace Company, if he saw something that, in process or product, could be improved, he made the suggestion to the management.

Here is a suggestion that he made for the construction of a warp truck that would assist in the moving of the heavy rolls of warp yarn from the storage shed to the lace machine. This is his freehand drawing where his artistic skill is apparent:

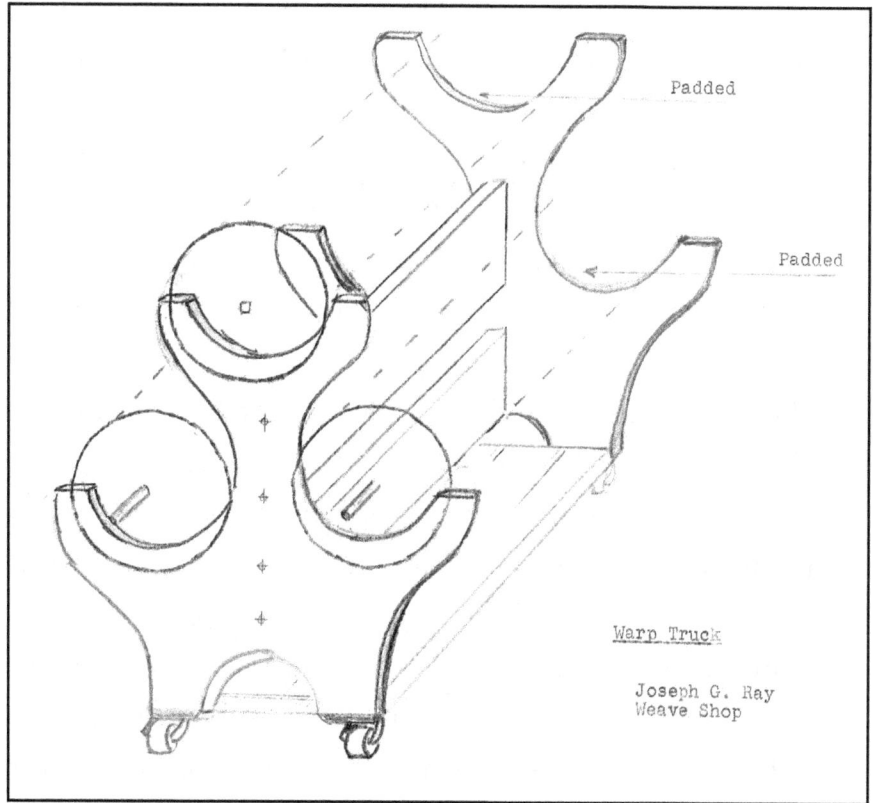

Recognizing his expertise and initiative, management made him an offer to take on a newly created position in "quality control." On a Valley Lace Company letterhead, the following announcement was made with a handwritten notation of the date 11/28/1966:

"In keeping with a policy of trying to promote from within the company ranks, we take pleasure in announcing the following appointment.
Joseph "George" Ray—will assume a newly created position in the Quality Control area.

(Signed) GR Bodell, Jr.
Valley Lace Co., Inc."

Needless to say, this was a great boost for my father. How wonderful to have his skills and worth acknowledged in this way! But what did it mean for our family? I was sixteen at the time and a junior in high school so quite self-centered and wrapped up in my own world, but I do remember it discussed between my parents that fall in hushed tones. I was not asked to weigh in on it, but I knew it was a momentous decision.

Working through the pros and cons as in any important decision, my father weighed the benefits versus the risks. The benefits certainly included an increased steady pay no longer dependent upon how many racks my father produced or even whether or not he worked. Even though my parents had been saving for my college education since my birth, predictable income would be welcome with college less than two years away for me. Also, it meant a certain measure of prestige and, thankfully, no more filthy graphite laden work clothes for my mother to wash on a daily basis. He could now wear a shirt, jacket and tie (clip-on tie only for safety around the moving parts of the machines) every day to work instead of overalls.

The disadvantages did not escape my father. He readily recognized that this position put him squarely in the "no man's land" of middle management, between the bosses who expected measurable improvements, and the workers with whom he had worked alongside, many of them family and friends, for so many years. Both those relationships would clearly change, and they did.

Moreover, it meant that by working in management that Dad was no longer a lace weaver and therefore no longer a member of the union, the Amalgamated Lace Operatives of America, Leavers Branch #7. It meant severing the working relationships that he had cultivated, and enjoyed, with some very fine individuals at the branch, section, and executive levels of the union; however, in the eyes of some of the regular rank-and-file workers, it was tantamount to treachery and put him in the enemy camp. Not all, but a few individuals took exception to his new position, and expressed their displeasure by dumping garbage on our front lawn, crank phone calls, and other dirty tricks that I'm sure were unknown to me.

Dad would not be cowed or deterred. He took the position that he could do his job for management by improving conditions for the workers. Rather than critiquing their work, which some had feared, he worked to create an environment that helped make them more productive and therefore put more money in their pockets. He felt that a happy workforce was a more productive workforce.

One example of this was the incentive pay program that he implemented for the threaders and winders, the women who were responsible for the critical job of inserting the yarn (thread) into the bobbins that filled the carriages in the machines. Another improvement was installing fans in the shops to alleviate the sweltering heat in the summer. He also researched and implemented the use of alternative compounds to graphite for the purpose of lubrication that were lighter in color, therefore causing less soiling and less wear and tear in the bleaching process.

Here is a diagram of his plan to improve the scouring and rinsing of the lace webs:

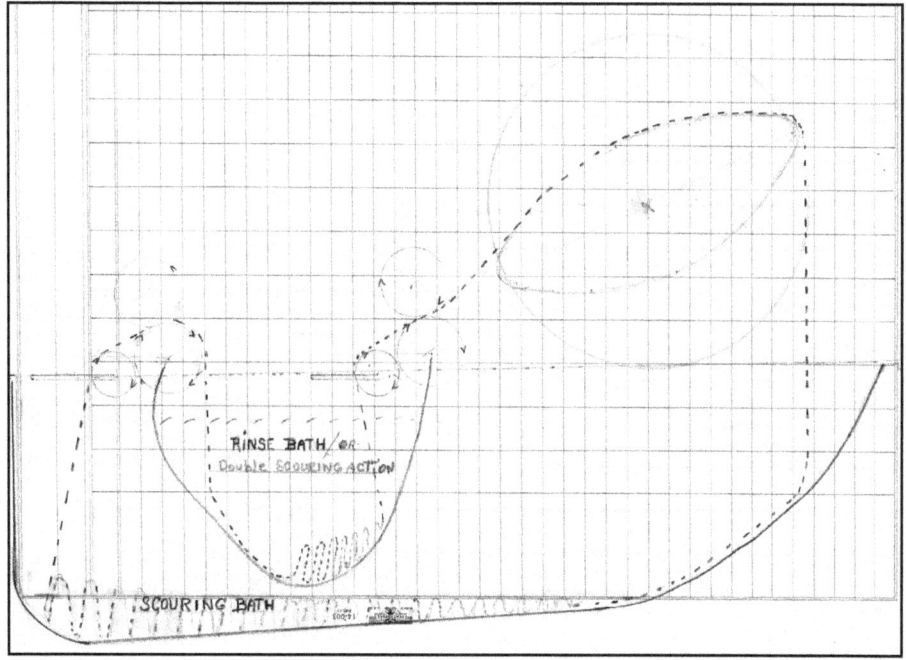

Dad's natural artistic talent is obvious from these few diagrams. There is no doubt that had he been allowed to stay in school and to pursue training as a draftsman, he would have been successful. Nevertheless, he used his talents wherever and whenever they could be applied in his working career and beyond for his own pleasure. He possessed a great imagination that served him well throughout his life.

Looking back on this opportunity in quality control, it occurs to me in retrospect that management might have had a hidden agenda in offering my father the position. On the face of it, it was obviously to their advantage to have someone of Dad's initiative and experience working in that role; however, Dad was becoming an active force in the trade union with his leadership becoming more apparent. In my opinion, and others may disagree, having Dad in the management camp was a way to "kill two birds with one stone" by not only improving manufacturing processes but also removing him as a force to be reckoned with in the union.

OWNERSHIP: FRONTIER MANUFACTURING COMPANY AND RAYBRO, INC.

The Valley Lace Company on Main Street in the village of Hope, town of Scituate, Rhode Island was the primary place of employment for the Ray brothers for decades. Valley Lace Company was incorporated as a domestic profit corporation in the State of Rhode Island on November 29, 1933. The President was Arthur M. Wiener, Chief Executive Officer of Wiener Laces, Inc. located on 295 Fifth Avenue, New York City, New York. All decisions pertaining to the management of the mill came from the Wiener family and Gilbert "Ronnie" Bodell, Jr. who was a director of the corporate board and took on the role of General Manager. Although the Rhode Island Secretary of State corporate database indicates that the corporation certificate was revoked in September of 1997, George's youngest brother, Tommy (94 years of age at this writing), recalls that operations at Valley Lace Company ceased sometime between 1970 and 1972.

While other businesses leased and used the physical space, the manufacture of lace D/B/A (doing business as) Valley Lace Company ceased to exist. This left the Ray brothers, and many others, without employment in the trade at which they had become experts. The brothers, ranging in age from fifty-four to forty-two, were still too young to retire. It was Dad's idea to go into business for himself or, at least, in partnership with another investor.

It is unclear how it all transpired because Dad destroyed many of the paper records relative to the two entities with which he was involved: 1) Frontier Manufacturing Company and 2) RayBro, Inc. As near as memory serves, a financial arrangement was made with Gilbert "Ronnie" Bodell, Jr. to start a lace manufacturing business at the previous location of Ronnie Lace Company in Coventry, Rhode Island. The specifics of that business arrangement are unknown to me, however, the Rhode Island Secretary of State corporations database records that Frontier Manufacturing was incorporated in the State of Rhode Island on February 5, 1975 with Gilbert R. Bodell, Jr. as Vice-President.

A photo taken at that site features a lace machine with the weaver at work identified as Dad's brother, Alfred. Indeed, Dad had made sure that his three brothers were employed at the factory as lace weavers. His youngest brother, Tommy, still recalls working there and that he partnered with his older brother, Frankie on a machine.

The caption inserted by Dad on the photo reads:

"This photo dates to 1978. It pictures my brother, Alfred, with his back to the camera conversing about the artisan's finer points of lacemaking. In co-founding Frontier Manufacturing, Inc. in February, 1975, I owned and managed a commanding interest in the corporation of twenty-seven employees. The operation of ten lace machines made demands of me, seven days a week, for nearly ten years."

Part Five:
Politics and Community Service

POLITICAL PHILOSOPHY

As long as I can remember, my father held conservative views. As a child growing up, I had little understanding of the difference between a Democrat and a Republican. My earliest memory of any political opinions in the household was during the reelection campaign of President Dwight D. Eisenhower in 1956 when I heard Dad proclaim, "I like Ike." (I would have been too young at the age of two to remember that campaign slogan during Ike's first presidential campaign in 1952.) It was a lilting little tagline that a five-year-old would have mimicked—and I did, probably partly to gain my father's favor. Looking back, it would have made sense that Dad would support Ike. After all, Dad served in the Army in Europe during World War II and Eisenhower was the supreme commander of allied forces in Western Europe. But there was more to it than that.

Politics was never discussed in the house between Mom, Dad, and me even though I recall heated arguments between Dad and his brother-in-law, my Uncle Louie, in my grandmother's house on more than one occasion. Life was a simple "Father Knows Best" scene in the '50s with clearly defined gender roles—Dad worked, Mom stayed home and took care of us and we had one car that only Dad drove.

As previously mentioned, Dad tried to teach Mom to drive on a standard transmission when I was still very small before the age of five. I remember standing up in the rear seat on the hump in the floor when a big white car pulled out from a side street right in front of Mom. She froze at the wheel coming face-to-face with the driver so that Dad had to quickly grab the wheel to avoid a crash. She was so shaken by the experience that it was years before she ever tried again. She never did get her driver's license.

We always ate supper at 5:00 p.m. on the dot when Dad worked the 6 a.m.–2 p.m. shift at the Valley Lace Company. After supper, he and I watched the evening news at 6:00 p.m. whether it was Walter Cronkite on CBS or the Huntley Brinkley Report on NBC. I never understood what it was all about until the 1960 Presidential campaign when there appeared a new face on the TV screen. I was not quite ten but the excitement that summer was palpable. We watched the televised presidential debates on the black and white television where this handsome young face dominated the screen. Compared to his shifty-eyed opponent with the 5 o'clock shadow, his charisma literally jumped off the screen and grabbed you. Moreover, he was from Massachusetts, neighbor to us in Rhode Island, and a Catholic! John Fitzgerald Kennedy was like the second coming in New England and many were all in.

When Kennedy won the nomination for President at the Democratic National Convention, Dad and I watched it all to the end. It was late when it finally ended but I was allowed to stay up because it was summer with no school the next day. I climbed the stairs to bed hearing the campaign song ringing out, "Going up to Wash-Ing-Ton to shake hands with President Kennedy..." I don't recall watching the Republican National Convention, so I guess we were...Democrats?

The Kennedys brought a new and fresh sense of excitement to the country. The young handsome President with his elegant wife who spoke fluent French and well-behaved young children were on the cover of LIFE and LOOK magazines every week. American women were soon all wearing pill box hats in the winter and lace mantillas in the summer to Mass on Sundays and to confession on Saturdays. Even during the Cuban missile crisis, as scary as those days in October of 1962 were, President Kennedy carried himself as a leader in control. His "vigah" (Bostonian for "vigor"), wit and energy were contagious and, did I mention he was the first Roman Catholic President? Certainly, that was a plus in my father's book.

Then, quite suddenly, the bubble burst when on a sunny day in November, 1963 in Dallas, Texas, President Kennedy was assassinated in the rear seat of a convertible limousine seated beside his elegant young wife wearing a rose pick suit with a matching pill box hat. The country was in shock and the mourning was pervasive. Cardboard prints of a presidential portrait of John F. Kennedy could be purchased at any store probably for a dollar. We bought one at Ann & Hope that Dad promptly placed it in an elegant dark wood frame, that I believe displaced a nondescript calendar print. It was hung prominently in the place of honor in the front hall of our two story, center hall Cape Anne colonial on Greene Street. Whether entering from the front door or the back, it was not to be missed. It was hung just above the small table that held the beige rotary telephone at the bottom of the hall stairs. I passed it every time I climbed and descended those stairs and stared at it while talking on the phone. It hung there from 1963 until the house was sold in July, 2004. So, I guess we were indeed Democrats?

My future in-laws certainly thought so. As I previously mentioned, I met David Fraley in 1970 while I was a student at the University of Rhode Island and Dave was stationed at Quonset Point in the U.S. Navy. Fast forward to the engagement in 1972, and Truth and Mack Fraley traveled to Rhode Island from southwest Virginia to meet the Rays.

Truth and Mack were staunch Republicans and had steeled themselves to meet the liberal, northern, Catholic prospective in-laws. Truth later said that as soon as she saw Kennedy's portrait so prominently displayed on first entering our home, that her suspicions (I won't say fears) were confirmed. It took a few drinks and frank conversations for them to find out that Dad was really quite conservative and a Republican to boot. So, we were... Republicans?

The framed portrait of President John F. Kennedy that hung in the foyer of our house at 50 Greene Street.

Despite his admiration for John F. Kennedy, Dad was indeed a registered member of the Republican party. In fact, he supported RI State Senator Donald Roch, a local Republican and Chairman of the Republican State Central Committee, and ran himself (although unsuccessfully) for Tax Assessor for the town of West Warwick on the Republican ticket. But beyond his declared partisan affiliation, Dad certainly agreed with many of the commonly held tenets of political conservatism.

If one agrees with a basic definition of political conservatism as a philosophy that is characterized by a belief in individual liberty, small government, low taxes, and fiscal responsibility, then Dad could check off all those boxes. Add to that list items such as a strong national defense, personal responsibility and self-reliance, and a belief in American exceptionalism, then I would say that in the '80s and beyond that Dad was certainly a Reagan Republican. In fact, in those years after his retirement, Dad became a fan and follower of Rush Limbaugh, listening religiously to the daily broadcasts on the radio. I know that Limbaugh's analysis of issues resonated with Dad as we would often listen together and discuss points in detail. I believe that it is safe to say that Dad was pleased that I shared his conservative political point of view for the most part. It certainly made for very pleasant visits later in his life with frank discussions without tiptoeing around the partisan political mine field, however, it was not always so.

I recall returning home in the summer of 1969 from my freshman year of college filled with the liberal notions that were poured in my ear over months of lectures in history and philosophy. In addition, I was breathing the very campus air that was imbued with the activism of the 60s. The civil rights movement, Women's Liberation and, of course, the Viet Nam War protests were front and center of almost any discussion in those days on any college campus. Rhode Island's flagship public institution of higher education was no exception. Despite its location in the sleepy little village of "Little Rest," Kingston, Rhode Island, the University of Rhode Island was quickly shifting from the traditions of wearing of the freshman "beanies" and pre-football game bonfires in 1968 when I matriculated to long hair and jeans, anti-war rallies, and campus appearances from the likes of Adam Clayton Powell and Timothy Leary by the time I graduated in 1972. Add to that the invasion of Cambodia and the killing of four Kent State students in May of 1970 and you have an unprecedented time of unrest.

My conversations with my father in those days were one-sided. He listened patiently while I raged against the machine, social injustice, and the need for more welfare programs. Of course, as the child of immigrants who weathered the Great Depression, a World War II veteran, and a self-made man, he must have wondered what sort of education his hard-earned money was funding. In fact, later in life looking back on those days, he said, "I thought I had lost you." Certainly, as the sheltered only child of a traditional Portuguese-American family, I was now exposed to many new, and some radical ideas, that I had neither the skills nor the experience to process and evaluate. My world view was still very narrow as I soaked up and internalized every new idea that came my way.

The swing of the pendulum eventually modified my outlook when I began to realize how much money was deducted from my own paychecks and I began to question how my hard-earned tax dollars were being used. Dad just smiled wisely and said, "Now do you see?" He liked to repeat the often-quoted Mark Twain reference, "When I was a boy of 14, my father was so ignorant I could hardly stand to have the old man around. But when I got to be 21, I was astonished at how much the old man had learned in seven years." Time is a great equalizer of things. Although we did not always agree on every point, I was grateful that we shared a common point of view in this area.

COMMUNITY SERVICE

On more than one occasion, I heard Dad say, "If I can't be part of the solution, then at least I can avoid being part of the problem." He believed strongly in being a useful contributor to society as opposed to being a detractor.

Dad's first foray into volunteerism, to my knowledge, was helping out at St. Anthony's Church, the Roman Catholic parish established for the Portuguese community in River Point in 1925. His service began the year that I entered second grade at St. Anthony's Parochial School, when an elderly nun needed a ride from the convent to the elementary school and back again each school day. It was only a ten minute walk of about a half mile in distance, but Sister Mary Dionysius, who was already quite elderly and severely stooped over with arthritis, could not manage it as the other younger nuns could.

Dad had made arrangements to car pool for rides to school with another lace weaver who lived near us and who worked the opposite shift. So it was arranged that my father would drive in the mornings, picking up the man's daughter and Sr. Dionysius and another nun (they always traveled in pairs) while his friend took the afternoon pick up at 3 p.m. The reverse would happen the following week alternating so on.

I was seated between my father and Sr. Dionysius on the wide front bench seat in the big green Nash. It certainly sets your day up to behave yourself riding to school between your father and a nun (also my third grade teacher) in the morning. On the flip side on alternate weeks, I had the hot seat on the ride home between them hoping there would be no negative reports about my behavior during the school day. Sometimes there were.

But his chauffeuring did not stop there. Because of her medical condition, Sr. Dionysius needed occasional visits to a doctor in Cranston. My father volunteered to drive them taking me along for the ride. While we were waiting, we'd stop in at a little diner on Park Avenue and have hot chocolate and a corn muffin. Dad always made the simplest things seem like the most awesome treat. I have savored corn muffins grilled with butter and spread with grape jelly ever since.

There is always much to do and a lack of funds with which to do them in a small immigrant parish. Immigration was experiencing a hiatus in the 1950s, so the Azorean immigrants already there for decades and their American born children were already quite integrated into American culture; however, they were not well-heeled. It was a working class group of parishioners but extremely hardworking and proud. If there was a lack of funds to donate to the church coffers, there was not a lack of able-bodied men to help with repairs and maintenance and women to cook for fundraising *"jantars"* (suppers) and *"festas"* (feasts). On more than one occasion, Dad was part of the group that donated its labor, scraping and painting the church, the convent, and the rectory on the exterior as well as an interior refresh when needed. The Portuguese believed it was a waste of money to pay for a job that you could do yourself. If they had little treasure, they donated their time and talent generously.

Before long my father was an active member, and then later President of the Holy Name Society. It was a men's organization at the church whose mission was to promote clean language by refraining from profanity or taking the Lord's name in vain. A weekend long fundraising "bazaar" took place in June that included every kind of traditional

Portuguese food, raffles, games, and rides. It was intense work but the proceeds would benefit the church. For Easter, my father established an Easter flower and candy sale by buying potted lilies, tulips, and hyacinths as well as pound boxes of chocolates at wholesale, then selling the wares at a profit again to benefit the church. The heady scent of flowers filled the church basement on Easter weekend when customers could stop by to pick up their orders. Every *"mãe"* (mother) in the parish had at least one potted Easter plant and a pound of chocolates from their children on that holiday. If she didn't receive one, it was a *"vergonha"* (shame) to have shirked one's filial duty on such a major holiday. In fact, my Ray grandparents ended up with five potted plants and five boxes of chocolates since not one of her children would be shown up by their siblings in the affection department.

Fundraising was only a sideline benefit of the Holy Name Society. The primary mission was to nurture the spiritual health of the men of the parish. From time to time, the group organized a retreat for the men at Our Lady of Peace Retreat Home in Narragansett, Rhode Island. Dad saved a photo and notes from just such a retreat in 1958 when fifty of the parish men attended.

This source material was provided by Dad to Amby Smith for an article in his "Seniors" column in the local *Kent County Daily Times* which was published on November 12, 1996. The article memorialized the occasion with a group photo of the men and quotes from Dad's observations:

> *"Men who were born during the years of 1895 to 1935, fifty in all, came together at the Our Lady of Peace Retreat Home in Narragansett back in 1958, in a prayerful celebration for the bountiful blessings of self and their families... The men went to Narragansett (recalling) a time in life which tested the mettle of one's character, (and) joining in thankful acclamation for their deliverance from the dark days of trials and tribulations...At the retreat, many of the elders spoke of turmoil during and after World War I. Others spoke of the roaring twenties of bootleggers and of crimes and passions consumed from the flow of alcohol. And, too, they spoke of the great depression which is said to have started in the East Coast area as early as 1927..."*

The names captioned in the group photo are all too familiar to me as they were fathers and grandfathers of many of my classmates at St. Anthony's School. Among the group are many of my own family members including: Ernest Simas (uncle), Joseph "George" Ray (father), Francis Ray (uncle), Thomas Ray (uncle), Louis Furtado (maternal grandfather), Anthony Ray (great uncle), David Dressel (uncle). This was the devout and tight knit community of men that my father served during his tenure as president of the Holy Name Society.

Dad's Holy Name Society Ribbon

FIRE STUDY COMMITTEE

For reasons never made known to me, fire safety held a special interest for my father. I never heard him voice why exactly because he had no particular expertise on the subject except to make comment that it was of the highest priority for the town's public safety.

Dad was a "worrier" by nature, always alert to head off mishaps before they might occur. "An ounce of prevention is worth a pound of cure" was one of his many mottos. Looking to avoid any disaster and improve safety in general, one of the first comments about fire safety that I recall had to do with the color of fire engines. He questioned why fire engines and rescue vehicles were painted red and not a more highly visible color, such as yellow. He observed, that given the speed with which these huge vehicles barrel down congested streets and through busy intersections, does it not make sense that they should be as visible as possible? Among his many clippings (he saved anything that caught his interest), I found an article entitled, "Call for Bright Yellow Firetrucks Has Many Firefighters Seeing Red" by Nichole M. Christian, Staff Reporter of the Wall Street Journal (1996). The article cited a study by Dr. Stephen S. Solomon that showed that yellow fire trucks were involved in less accidents than red fire trucks. Once again it would seem that Dad was ahead of his time.

Never shy about voicing his concerns on matters of public concern, his views must have been noted. In 1969, the West Warwick Town Council adopted a resolution to establish a fire study committee to determine the needs of the municipal fire department. Dad was included in the committee. The final report was submitted in November, 1969 recommending three new pumper trucks and the building of a new three-bay fire station on Cowesset Avenue in Crompton.

Apparently, the recommendations of the fire study committee were slow to be executed much to Dad's dismay. The following Letter to the Editor was published in the *Pawtuxet Valley Times* voicing his concern.

> "Letter to the Editor: 'Let's do what has to be done.'
>
> To paraphrase a South of the border cliché, "Tomorrow is soon enough for me." It seems that the West Warwick Fire Department has suffered too many tomorrows and too many delays due to financial and rhetorical logjams.

At long last we have three new pumpers and in the very near future expect the arrival of an aerial ladder truck. However, the problem is that we are not quite sure of a place to house such a large piece of equipment on the delivery date. We should now get on with the next order of priority, i.e. the building of the new Crompton Fire Station.

Since its 1947 inception, the attitude of the Fire Department has been good considering the equipment they had to work with. How they have managed to hold any semblance of fire protection for the town's citizenry under past conditions and equipment failures is a miracle in itself. Surely, this kind of loyalty and dedication warrants a measure of respect and praise.

Oh, how many times have we heard the fire alarm sound in the wee hours of the morning and rolled over in our sleep confident that Chief Pryor and his men would gain control over the situation. Ask how many accident victims who have suffered pain, shock, and confusion speak of their gratitude for the merciful helping hands of our rescue squad. It is human that we quickly forget these important services.

It is also human, on occasion, to take stock of our service assets and place a value on them. The more congested we become population-wise, the more we feel the need for municipal services.

Through a resolution adopted in 1969 by the Town Council, there was set in motion the formulation of the Fire Study Committee to study the Fire Department needs of our community. The Committee consumed many months of exhaustive study and research and presented to the Council its findings in November of 1969. The summation of that report was succinct and to the point. It stated what the Department needs are, what the estimate {sic} cost would be and a schedule to implement these priorities. The study and presentation of the report was simple, uncomplicated, without fanfare, political or otherwise.

Now again in trouble waters, we are experiencing another logjam. A leading dedicated and respected citizen has withdrawn from his offer to act as Building Agent due to ramifications unknown. A man, who in the opinion of many regarding the building and construction trade, rates second to none.

Moreover, there is no one (in the opinion of this writer) who is more knowing in the expertise of fire equipment and fire containment than Chief Pryor. It would be refreshing and pleasing to the ear to have Chief Pryor delegate his program over contrary voices by saying, 'This is what we need. This is the available money and time we have to do it in. Let's get on and do what has to be done.'"

J. George Ray
50 Greene St.
West Warwick

In 1971 the citizens of West Warwick approved a bond measure for $295,000. These funds were used to purchase three new Maxim Pumpers, a ladder truck and to add an addition to station 3. Also included in these funds was the construction of a new station 4 on Cowesset Avenue in Crompton. The new three bay station replaced the considerably smaller, single bay station on Main Street which was originally built in 1893 to house the Crompton Hose Company.[xxxvii] A plaque mounted on the wall of Station #4 dates the dedication of the station in 1972.

Dad was very proud of his contribution in accomplishing these much needed services for the town, especially the construction of the new fire station, Engine 4, on Cowesset Avenue. Thirty years later, the critical need for that fire station was driven home, when Engine 4 was the first responder on the scene of the tragic Station Nightclub Fire on February 20, 2003.

According to the Report of the Technical Investigation of The Station Nightclub Fire, "note the location of Fire Station #4 at 110 Cowesett Avenue about 500 m (1650 ft) to the west of The Station." A time analysis of the onset, rapid spread, and emergency response shows that Engine 4 arrived on the scene less than four minutes of being dispatched.[xxxviii] Unfortunately, the combination of highly flammable sound insulation, pyrotechnics, and poor egress in an overcrowded venue resulted in an overwhelmingly chaotic situation even for those quick first responders on the scene. A total of one hundred people lost their lives and two hundred and thirty were injured in the second deadliest fire in New England, second only to the Cocoanut Grove fire in Boston, in 1942 which resulted in four hundred and ninety-two deaths.[xxxix]

Even during Dad's last years while in residence in assisted living at The Villa at St. Antoine's in North Smithfield, fire safety continued to be an interest of his. Recognizing that we could now search almost any topic on the internet and print out documents, he asked me to find articles on the Cocoanut Grove Fire of November 28, 1942 in Boston, MA and The Station Nightclub Fire of February 20, 2003 in West Warwick. I printed them out and started a binder for him that he studied in detail.

Dad was not living at The Villa very long before he was meeting with the facility's administrator about a potential fire hazard that he found worrying. As a Roman Catholic institution, the residents of The Villa could attend Mass on Sunday mornings. It was held in an activity room ordinarily used for seated exercise for the elderly, but on Sundays it was the setting for Mass in front of an impromptu altar with rows of folding chairs. Dad observed that the room was filled to capacity with residents, the majority of whom used walkers for assistance, and that the small room had only one door on a short corridor to the main lobby. His concern was that if a fire broke out, possibly from open flame candles on the altar, that the ability of elderly, mobility-challenged people, mostly using walkers, would create a logjam during an evacuation. It was not long before the Fire Marshal was brought in and the venue for Sunday Mass relocated to the large and spacious dining room with multiple points of egress out of the building.

THE GOOD SAMARITAN

There is no doubt in my mind that there are probably many untold occasions when others benefitted from Dad's generous heart. I know, too, that he would never want to be recognized or praised for such acts of kindness.

Nevertheless there was one occasion that he mentioned, not to draw attention to himself but to wonder what happened to the man that he helped. As he told it, it was a cold dark winter morning at about 5:30 a.m. when Dad was driving on Fairview Avenue on his way to start work at 6:00 a.m. at the Valley Lace Company in Hope. Driving down that dark road with no other cars in sight at that hour, he spotted the form of a man draped over a fire hydrant on the sidewalk on the right side of the road. He didn't hesitate to stop, pulling up next to him to assess the man's condition from inside the car. Determining that this was a person in trouble, he got out to see what was wrong. There were no visible injuries nor signs of alcohol but the man's breathing was shallow and he was pale.

"What's the matter, Mac?" asked Dad, falling into Army parlance. The man could hardly talk. With no pay phone nearby (and long before cell phones), Dad judged that the best move would be to take him directly to the Fire Station in Phenix as the closest point of medical attention. Helping him into his car, it was only five minutes to the station where he immediately found fire and rescue staff on duty. "Don't worry, sir," they said, "We'll take it from here." Leaving the man in capable hands, he went on his way to work. He never knew what happened to the fellow only hoping that he made a difference that day.

Part Six:
Musings

———•♦•———

Retirement at the age of sixty came far too early for my father. Still in good health with an active mind and sufficient energy, he found it difficult to sit still for long. Relaxing or just puttering around the house did not suit him and, certainly, being underfoot as my mother went about her usual rhythm of daily chores was not working. "George, you retired too early," I'd hear her frequently say.

During the winter months, there was no escape except to the basement where he took to wood carving primitive cars at first for his grandsons, but later more challenging figures of horses. Dad also created props for my Byer's Carolers Christmas display out of scrap wood. He made sidewalks with fences, lamp posts, and front doors (some replicating those to our own homes) around which the singing Victorian figures could be arranged. He actually became quite good at carving and woodworking. He pursued that pastime until the onset of Parkinson's Disease when the resulting hand tremors made it too difficult to execute what he envisioned.

When the weather allowed, he took to taking long walks around the streets of West Warwick, often with his younger brother, Tommy, with whom he forged a special bond at this point in their lives. It was good exercise, got him out of the house, and was therapeutic for the stiffness of Parkinson's Disease. It was then that, I believe, his active imagination took flight. While his feet and legs wandered the streets of town, so did his mind and his imagination. Arriving home, he sought to capture his thoughts on paper putting a newly purchased Brother word processor to work. He started writing, sometimes poetry of light-hearted moments from his childhood, but at other times, abstract and dark musings that he struggled to get down in words.

He often expressed frustration at not being able to communicate his thoughts. He wanted feedback from me and reassurance that he was being understood. Sometimes I didn't quite get it so he would explain what he meant. Some of his writings were published in the form of letters to the editor or in the "Poetry Corner" of the *Kent County Daily Times*. Amateur critics can be brutal and he despaired that "they just don't get it." It was more important to me that HE "got it" and was "getting it down." As so often in his life, his insights were far ahead of his time in his premonitions of things to come.

After a while, he became a contributor of ideas and source material to Ambrose "Amby" Smith's[xi] "Seniors" column in the *Kent County Daily Times*. Amby Smith had previously been sports editor and Vice-President of the paper's predecessor, the *Pawtuxet Valley Daily Times*, for forty years. Of course, it was Amby's column and he had the by-line, but he credited Dad as a source and quoted his comments and text often. For a man, who did not even finish the tenth grade in high school and built his own vocabulary by reading everything he could find and studying—yes, studying—the dictionary, he was quite proud of this accomplishment. While I believe that he never looked for praise, it was honest feedback and recognition of his efforts that were most important to him.

When Dad entered assisted living at the Villa at St. Antoine's, it wasn't long before his writing ability was recognized. Many of his pieces were included in the monthly Villa newsletter. The nostalgic themes of his youth and "good ol' days" resonated with many of the residents. He enjoyed sharing his work with some of the residents and some of them shared theirs in kind. I believe that they developed a small and informal literary group where members shared their work which gave my father great enjoyment.

Even though he recognized that times were hard during the Great Depression and World War II, he often waxed nostalgic in his writings longing for simpler times when love of God, country, and family as well as values of decency were the norm. I know that he feared for the future and the direction in which he saw society heading…and with good reason.

YEARN FOR THE RADIO DAYS

Radio, the prime entertainment of yesteryear,
Enjoyed by count were few.
The Majestic was the radio of choice,
Not expensive when purchased new.
A cathedral-shaped box, with two knobs on the front,
With a lighted dial to see,
And were you gainfully employed with one at home,
You were luckier than most would be.

When reception was poor in bad weather,
Interference and static took its toll.
An antenna was strung some fifty feet,
From the corner of the house to a pole.
On a winter's evening, when the wind blew cold,
All huddled around by the fire,
Or in the still of the night laying in our beds,
You could hear the hum of the wire.

It was a time reminiscent of the family Waltons,
With love of family we saw,
When respect for parents and elders,
And a high regard for the law.
Those were the simpler times,
When honesty was assumed to be,
You could leave your home with doors unlatched,
Without need for lock and key.

Aunt Theresa and Joe were the first that I know,
To own this electronic media.
It was a gray metal box, that transmitted sound,
Through a large cone-shaped speaker.
And on a hot summer night, kids gathered to play,
Beneath an old corner pole light,
We were told to behave, so grown-ups could hear,
The World's Heavyweight Championship fight.

Radio, then, was not a means of abuse,
Or to repeat social travails.
It was a form of news reported,
Entertainment and promotional sales.
And never a word spoke off color,
Or of a program censored for fear,
That voices sent through the airways,
Would grate on innocent ears.

Kudos for that radio programming,
When there was never a cause for debate,
When reporting the news was an event of the day,
And not a story to make.
Recalling times past of love and sharing,
And walking the nights unafraid,
Dare who care, though silent in prayer,
Wish we were back in the radio days.

– Joseph "George" Ray, December, 1993

A COMMENTARY ON MONETARY

This story in verse relates to two bottles of nickels given to grandchildren with a subtle caveat to invest.

> Many years ago in the thirties,
> A nickel could buy one plenty,
> A bottle of pop or a doughnut to sop,
> In a big five cent cup of coffee.
>
> It could also buy a five cent cigar,
> As a gift to your grand old Daddy,
> And in addition too, you could buy brand new,
> A yo-yo called a Jim Dandy.
>
> A nickel back then was handsome to spend,
> On a candy bar to share with your sweetie,
> And that same candy bar had plenty to share,
> Unlike the ones now so teeny.
>
> The nickels imprisoned in bottles, one sees,
> Will accrue not buried like pirate's treasure,
> It reminds one though, as currencies go,
> How inflation has reduced it in measure.
>
> Moral: An exercise in principles will accrue interest from principals.
>
> – Joseph "George" Ray, West Warwick

AMBULATING AT SUNRISE

The following is a commentary of a vision in my mind's eye while walking at early sunrise.

A shaft of light peers through my window,
Beckons me to early rise,
Body rigid from evening's slumber,
Gestures a need to exercise.

Dressed to meet the morning drill,
Disheveled though resigned,
Greeting not yet the sunrise,
Ambulating sylvan avenue's incline.

Straining body sinews, rebuking atrophy,
Yet, slow in gait I must seem,
Pausing moments not to rest,
In wonderment partaking nature's scenery.

Damp the earth from recent rain,
Freshens more sweet breath of air,
Foraging raven, robins and songbirds, too,
Free, not in flight, dauntless though I'm there.

East, Northeast, glows now a trumpeting sunrise,
Bright so, dulling vision with glaring fee,
Clouds of azure, reds of orange, adorn angelus skies,
As shafts of brilliance, spear through leafy trees.

Halted again by sounds of songbirds,
Heard the cooing of the mourning dove,

Sparkle pondlets of still mirrored waters,
Reflecting images from above.

The early risers greet the morning,
Commuters in hurried meter, in clattered sound,
Move as if there's no tomorrow,
Seeing not the wondrous beauty all around.

And if per chance when time permits,
You pause to gaze just once again,
To view nature's beauty that surrounds us,
Of a painted masterpiece of GOD'S realm.

– Joseph "George" Ray, West Warwick
Appeared in the "Poetry Corner," Kent County Daily Times.

ON NUDISM

This story in verse is an introspective that arose from a conversation with a former female employee who related her experience as a member of a nudist camp at Moonstone Beach.

To venture upon a colony of nudists,
Brings societal ambivalence to mind,
Among people of apparel abstinent,
Harkens back to biblical times.

Surely one may wonder,
Of the benefits of a choice free of care,
In concert with the era of Adam and Eve,
With nary a fig leaf to wear.

Free from conventional norm,
One views with enigma,
To be devoid of clothing,
If not dressed for dinner.

On a positive note,
Grant a degree of concession,
When retiring at bedtime,
There's no need for undressing.

When asked why nudity, replied she,
An uninhibited body gives freedom to the mind,
And maintains a sense of dignity,
Those in clothing rarely find.

– Joseph "George" Ray, January, 1996

ONCE A BEGGAR

Troubled by a recurring dream, a squire recalls his once pauperized life, when enslaved by an addiction but with perseverance and purity of purpose regains wealth and respectability.

Awakened by morning light,
From slumber in a marketplace,
My head rests on a curb of stone,
In restless nightmare a past I trace.

I know not what the morrow brings,
Naught have I a penny earned nor loaned,
Nor seek to plunder thy neighbor's realm,
Nor of little comfort to call a home.

Part Six: Musings

I trudge over country wide,
And come upon a beggar's cup to share,
Of tattered raiment once proudly worn,
I've reached a point to grin and bear.

I with no one but me to fault,
I was the beggar with shoeless feet,
I was the man with no food to eat,
I was the man on homeless streets.

I was that man who once stood tall,
I was that man who lost it all,
I, the beggar in tattered clothes,
I, once a squire steeped in lore.

Again, perchance to wander in slumber,
A cast in life weak with hunger,
Of tattered clothes held in scorn,
Recall I, a squire, no longer a wanderer.

– Joseph "George" Ray, October 30, 1996

Entering assisted living after a few months living with my husband and me was extremely difficult for my parents who were so fiercely independent all their lives. It wasn't long before they came to recognize that, as much as I wished to care for them myself, it was becoming too difficult for me to do so, especially as their medical needs increased. The Villa at St. Antoine's is a beautiful well-run facility, under the Roman Catholic Diocese of Providence, but it was not the home that they had created for themselves and loved for forty-nine years.

There are pros and cons to communal living, but my father, being a highly sociable person, made friends easily. Dad liked to laugh and joke, especially with the staff. In particular, there was a waitress employed part time at the Villa named Tara, a college student majoring in English, who took an interest in Dad and his writings. He would provide her with copies which she faithfully read and would return with the most thoughtful and insightful comments, signing them "Waitress Extraordinaire." That such a young woman could not only appreciate his work but, more importantly, grasp some of his more abstract notions, gave him no end of pride.

At the end of one of her detailed letters, she wrote:

> *"I used to think that you were a comedian, then I found out you're a noble historian, then I discover that you have a zest for writing poetry, then I read about your thoughts and feelings about meteorology, and I believe you are a scientist. I gave up trying to label you as one thing and determined that you are a modern day Renaissance Man. It seems almost ironic because your father told you to find your niche when you are very knowledgeable in a variety of fields. I was very enlightened by reading all your work..."*

Her interest and demonstration that she "got it" reinforced Dad's confidence in ways as an objective outsider that I never could as his daughter. I will be forever grateful for her sincere appreciation of his work and her friendship during the time that their paths crossed at that difficult point in his life.

RETROSPECT

> *Oh, how the dissolution of time,*
> *Tends to erase the mind,*
> *As hands become less steady*
> *And focus and sounds decline.*
>
> *For this is the price,*
> *We must pay as the toll,*
> *As we move down life's highway,*
> *Of the graying and the old.*

Yesterday has come and gone,
Enjoyed was a day of splendor,
Rejoice the morrow, a new dawning,
Again as sunset enjoins surrender.

Cope we must with social change,
Acceleration of time we scorn,
Say we, who lament the good old days,
In truth, the loss of youth we mourn.

Were I asked,
The second time around,
I would seek to cultivate,
These wondrous sights and sounds.

I would stop to view the beauty,
Which Nature has decreed,
And treat with reverence, this country mine,
Whose care was placed in thee.

I would contribute solutions,
To problems we've plenty of,
And keep in order our earthly home,
Forever clean and loved.

– *Joseph "George" Ray, September, 1995*

THE WONDERFUL MATRIX OF LIFE

With thoughts about pregnancy

A feel of oneness in a sphere,
In insulated slumber,
Transitory in developing time,
Imparting restless serene slumber.

A soft and fragile heart beats,
Echoes within my chamber,
Igniting fires of life,
Fertility of nature's fecund ember.

Absent solitude of oneness,
An inuring sound repeats,
What was alone in my chamber,
Within me now two hearts beat.

Tranquil in gestation interlude,
Maternal manifestations yearn,
Nourishing mind and body,
Bringing life's miracle to term.

With hope and love in one's heart,
In joyful anguish garner,
Nurtured for all times to come,
Go forth and hold a place of honor.

– Joseph "George" Ray, October 13, 1996

The following was published in the March, 2008 newsletter of The Villa of St. Antoine Assisted Living Community.

SEINING THE DEPTHS OF KNOWLEDGE

The rhythm of earth's ecology is so fine yet so complex. We mere mortals search to learn of its mysteries resting deep within its oceans.

> *In the streams of knowledge,*
> *Is where I choose to fish.*
> *Eagerly I cast my line,*
> *To angle erudition past remiss.*
>
> *As twilight draws ever near,*
> *And shadows long are cast,*
> *As a piscator, I sein my net,*
> *To harvest words, ever more to last.*
>
> *Navigating Neptune's passage,*
> *In sea and oceans, profusion ply.*
> *Bountiful life in waters deep,*
> *Adds mystery to time and tide.*
>
> *In multitude, creatures fleetness flow,*
> *Joined in aquatic symphonic reap,*
> *In academic pursuit of letters,*
> *A masterpiece mortals forever seek.*
>
> *– Joseph "George" Ray, September, 1996*

SHADOWS IN DECLINE

A shadow cast by daylight sun,
Stretches out as twilight nears,
Another day has come and gone,
So too, a week, a month, a year.

Oh, that I might halt,
This relentless pace of time,
To capture stillness in photo lens,
Events reviewed of yours and mine.

For time makes no apology,
It's one of nature's crimes,
Robbing us of youthfulness,
As advancing years decline.

What is past is prologue,
Time never to repeat again,
A photo print of days gone by,
Give testament of us back then.

So as sun and daylight dim,
With shadows in decline,
By capturing these precious moments,
We bring a halt to time.

– Joseph "George" Ray, In the summer of '95

CYCLE IN TIME, LENGTH OF ETERNITY

Synopsis: From rivulets to the depths and profusion of ocean waters, recycled into heaven's vaporous breast, in life a kindred comparison develops. From our first breath of life, we flow onward through the streams of growth. Within varied phases of maturity and engendered procreation life goes on, ultimately surrendering our last tribute in the cycle of life.

Much likened to a drop of water that has arisen from the sea and in a shower has fallen into a puddle, then drifts into a brook, finds its way into a stream, onward into a river, winding through obstructions of rocks and fallen trees, reaching the boundless sea from which it first rose. This microcosm of water in becoming one with the sea has lost its individuality.

>   From falling rain a river flows,
>   Rivulets to still lake waters shimmering sublime,
>   Confluence of rapids roaring to cascading falls,
>   Infusing aqueous profusion in swift decline.
>
>   Forging onward in predestined journey,
>   Unrelenting, rivers flow replete,
>   Filling estuaries of life's manna,
>   Come to rest in ocean's saline deep.
>
>   Urged as if by reticent command,
>   The salmon stir in agitated yearning,
>   Beckoning to waters fresh in spawning,
>   Depositing roe never more returning.

Organic cells in cyclical repletion,
Radiance absorbing vapors so fine,
Ascending heaven's gossamer breast,
Descending earthward by infinite Divine.

Thus, be it told: A cycle in life is short in time,
though in afterlife, an eternity.

– Joseph "George" Ray

INTROSPECTIVE OF THE HOLOCAUST

In his later years, when memories began to flow along with his words on paper, Dad would reflect more and more about his wartime experiences. Seared into his senses and mind were the scenes he encountered during the liberation of the concentration camps in Germany. He was forever haunted by that horrific evidence of man's inhumanity to man. The following reflection on that time was submitted to the *Kent County Daily Times* and published in Letters to the Editor, March 31, 1998:

"Walking at early sunrise, I find a contrasting but discordant strain between melodious birds of song and the raven. And, wondered I, what if absent birds of song only the raven survived?

Recalling before the war when prosperous Jews inhabited Germany, they were later subjected to inhumane treatment by Nazism. The following depicts an introspective of the Holocaust, where many Jews struggled for life, sustained by rancid food and a crust of bread.

For the many who suffered and survived the Holocaust, and of the Six Millions [sic] souls whose voices were the tones of perished agony, absent birds of song, would the cawing raven sound as sweet? (But through the grace of God we, too, could be one of you.)

Part Six: Musings

A TIME WHEN RAVENS SING

A discordant note is bittersweet,
When absent melodious strains,
The raven takes center stage,
When no longer, birds of sweet refrain.

Perched high atop a lifeless oak,
This ebony bird in flight soars,
An ungainly fowl with reddish eyes,
His beguiling songs a burden bore.

But upon the shoals and banks of time,
As storms and tides erode earth away,
When song birds are no longer heard,
The fiery red-eyed raven stays.

Or when Armageddon made its final play,
And fires of battle are ashes deep,
When absent melodious birds of song,
Would the cawing raven sound as sweet?

– *Joseph "George" Ray, West Warwick*

P.S. The writer took part in the liberation of concentration camps in Germany and Austria during World War II."

The above poem was one of those that Dad submitted, and was published in Letters to the Editor, that people told him that they simply did not understand. The piece is obviously full of symbolism set against the backdrop of the terror of Nazism that he personally witnessed. It is clearly there for anyone familiar with history to see. Certainly, the preface explains the direction in which the writer intended to take the reader as both a reminder of history and a cautionary tale for the future. Nevertheless, Dad wrote a commentary explaining further the thoughts that struck him when inspired by that cawing raven on his early morning walk.

"COMMENTARY: A TIME WHEN RAVENS SING

If we fail to learn from past mistakes, we are certain to repeat them. The threads of aging weave for some of us a clear tapestry of events past. I believe, however, that recall is sometimes a betrayer of accuracy when visions of vile events, too traumatic to face, are dimmed by the passing of time. Nevertheless, I feel compelled to write on this topic, not from melancholy, but to speak out about the ugliness that I experienced during a period of infamy in Europe.

The poem, "A Time When Ravens Sing," is a view I entertained while walking at sunrise, of the antithesis between the maleficent raven and melodious songbirds. I found myself reaching far into the recesses of my psyche to recall a period in my past that has now revisited itself and caused me to write about despicable acts of inhumane treatment. The poem may in appearance give little voice to the tragedies of the Holocaust; however, as an allegorical poetic concept it comes from deep within me that I offer the dichotomy between good and evil. The spirit of songbirds of love and peace versus the loathsome vulture fostering hate and deprivation.

First stanza: The raven, a descendant of the condor (vulture) is a symbol of maleficence standing watch over its domain as when Hitler came into power, as when he stripped the Jewish population of their property rights.

Second stanza: Hitler took control of their freedom of movement, "perched high atop a lifeless oak," enforced by the Gestapo, Germany's secret police.

Third stanza: Relates to genocide, the systematic killing of people, the result of moral decay, and the erosion of human rights and values "as storm and tides erode earth away."

Lastly: Armageddon, the final conflict between the forces of good and evil as well as the reference to the Four Horsemen of the Apocalypse, are the allegorical figures of the sixth chapter of the Book of Revelation. The horsemen, riding horses of different colors, are thought to symbolize power of conquest (white), violence or war (red), poverty or famine (pale), and death (black).

Had not the United States intervened in World War II with England, France, and Russia in defeating Germany, Japan, and Italy chances are that "for the grace of God" we too could have been among those who suffered and perished, and of the multitudes who continue to suffer in undeveloped countries under totalitarian rule. As so it goes..."

LIFE IS A STAGE

Oh, to be morally perfect in every respect,
And harbor no shame or deeds I regret,
To be a person of virtue, a human should be,
Would be rare in a few, not found in me.
To do my best in all I may do,
To be dedicated, and to oneself, be true,
And looked upon with love and compassion,
Judged not by my past, manifest by my actions.

The face in the mirror I daily see,
Reflects a challenge worthy to be,
In life's journey, a step at a time,
Looms a horizon, and mountains to climb.

A spirited face adds testament of content,
Of yesterday's anguish, no longer resentment,
I'm as good as some, not better than most,
What I've accomplished, I seek not to boast.

If life is stage, a thespian I am,
Promoting a character I know is a sham,
To be looked upon as a person of guile,
Be it raconteur, a bon vivant, or a person of style.

> *Oh, that I were perfect, such a bore would I be,*
> *Might friends take cover at first sight of me.*
> *If life is a stage, an actor I'm not,*
> *I like the person I am, not the person I'm not.*
>
> – Joseph "George" Ray, A Penitent
>
> Published in the April, 2008 newsletter of The Villa at St. Antoine Assisted Living Community.

WHY CREATION AND A REASON FOR LIVING

It is said that "brevity is the soul of wit." For what is to follow, this obviously does not apply. For how does one expect to succeed or even approach this topic expecting a short brief reply?

No doubt it begs the universal question, Who is responsible in the making of these worldly wonders that abound? With my limited cerebral capacity, I can only contemplate:

Is it like shouting from the highest mountaintop, or casting about the ocean blue, or crying out in the wilderness? What wonders has Nature brought of creatures large and small, these bountiful gifts made for you and me! The answer is embraced in the heart and soul of man.

Chapter 1

> *We are but raindrops in a universal sea,*
> *Like kindred molecules in a cycle of infinity.*
> *We exist in nature's realm as living matter,*
> *To be interned without treasures gathered.*
>
> *We live a life span from young to old,*
> *And await the call of bells that will toll,*
> *But apart from God's creatures large and small,*
> *We take comfort in the knowledge we were given a soul.*

The soul is a spirit that no one can see,
It lives in the body that God gave to me,
It feels pain in sorrow and joy in our laughter,
It's a compass in life to find the hereafter.

When given a soul, it was given anew,
How you use it in life will be up to you,
Good is the energy which increases in strength,
Temptation is the evil that leads to contempt.

Remember, too, faith in life plays a big part,
It reinforces our spirit when all is in doubt.
Hope is the beacon in life's journey we follow,
And may your conscience make choices for a blessed tomorrow.

So with faith, hope, and a reason for living,
I pray to the Lord that my sins be forgiven,
And what value a man who is sinful and bold,
Who gains riches and fame, but loses his soul.

Chapter 2

In conclusion, I add a post script,
In my mind's eye of what is to be,
It's an unfortunate dilemma,
With some inconvenience for you and me.

It's an unavoidable conclusion,
That one day one must do,
To go from chapter one of living,
One must die for chapter two.

Remember that life is just one damn thing after another.
It's temporary, so do it well and feel better.

– Joseph "George" Ray, November 9, 1993

My mother and her sister, Eileen, both passed away on the same day within hours of each other on April 29, 2008. That double shock had quite an impact on Dad. Even though my mother, needing skilled care and lived at the nursing facility while my father was at the assisted living facility on the same campus of St. Antoine's, he visited her frequently. Her loss left him quite adrift after sixty years of marriage.

The photo on the wall.
Has no voice to recall.
Memories great and small.
A wink and a smile tell it all.

Joseph G. Ray, August 23, 2011

Poem by Dad to commemorate her birthday following her passing.

Part Six: Musings

There is no doubt that thoughts of Dad's mortality weighed heavily upon him in his last years. His later writings are clearly filled with symbolism and allegories of the meaning of life. Ever the planner, he left the following for us as his last wishes. The poem may have been adapted from others popularly published.

"I am not at ease in writing the following, however necessary, I will.

My obituary: I, Joseph George Ray, a lifelong resident of West Warwick, son of the late Frank J. Ray and Mary Farias Ray, (name of survivors), request a private and simple funeral with no viewing. It could be mentioned that I served in the military in Europe during World War II. Beyond that my past will cease to be of importance except to those who love me and those I loved in turn. Date of Birth: January 29, 1924 in a little cottage known as 60 Wakefield Street, now numbered 95, of which much has changed over the years in landscape and residents. In spite of changes, and the passing of time, the memory of one's place of birth will forever be without change. Because the human brain is a wonder in retention of memories, time cannot change one's place of birth.

I would appreciate this poem to be read over me at my passing.

WHEN I MUST LEAVE YOU

When I must leave you,
    for the time has come.
Please do not grieve,
    and shed wild tears.
And hug your breast in sorrow
    throughout ensuing years.
But start out bravely,
    with a gallant smile.
And for my sake,
    and in my name.

Live on and do,
    all things the same.

Feed not your loneliness,
    on empty days,

But fill each working hour,
    in useful ways.

Reach out your hand,
    in comfort and cheer.

And heaven in turn will comfort you
    and hold you near.

Though precious life we find,
    must end in time,

For it comes to all,
    by GOD'S design.

    – Joseph G. Ray, May 27, 1996"

Dad survived my mother by almost four years. Although those were years of progressive debilitation due to Parkinson's Disease, his mind was incredibly sharp. He became interested in the Prophecies of Nostradamus asking me to Google and print information for him to study. On my visits, we would talk of all manner of things for which he would have endless questions. Once he saw that I could search information on my smartphone while sitting in front of him, he was energized to learn more. "Look this up on your decoder, will you?" We still call our personal cell phones "decoders" today, smiling and remembering him when we do.

Afterword

"The mind is a congenial filter…" For George Ray, it certainly was. Observing the breadth and depth of his interests, it is amazing to me how his mind filtered so many varied and intriguing suggestions into ideas. Both by nature and by experience, he was sharp, insightful, witty, resourceful, curious, and kind, among so many other qualities and used those as the filters through which he saw and formulated his values, attitudes, and worldview.

In the process of sorting through his papers, what was striking to me in organizing his works and the material for this book, was not only the finished pieces but the scraps, the notes, the scribbles, and the clippings. There were endless clippings relating to all manner of topics. For example, he was an avid reader of editorials by Brian Dickinson, a former chair of the *Providence Journal's* editorial department whose ten-year battle with Lou Gehrig's disease (ALS) attracted national attention.

Dad found great inspiration in Mr. Dickinson's writings. It was not only because of the writer's courageous battle with ALS, but because of his clear, succinct style and the topics he discussed. From over the twenty clippings Dad collected, there were: "Americans must not neglect their global responsibilities," "Giving thanks for our lives, individuality and memories," "Military scandals: Sorry display of slipping journalism standards," "International community shows hesitation in face of genocide," "Who says time is constant?" "Pondering the imagination," and "The challenge of prosecuting crimes against humanity." All of these would not only resonate with Dad but drive him into deeper thinking.

There were so many more clippings by other writers, such as: "Does true greatness demand crises?" by Robert J. Samuelson, "But how could a cell evolve?" by Michael J. Behe, "Immortal words, if we just read them," by David Shi. In addition there was a file about the Hale-Bopp Comet, the Cashless Society, and the Prophecies of Nostradamus. The topics were so varied from the scientific to the historic to the economic and more. When Tara Finlay, Waitress Extraordinaire at the Villa at St. Antoine's, said that Dad was a modern Renaissance Man, she may have been on to something.

Most surprising to me, however, was a Letter to the Editor to the Providence Journal entitled "The Portuguese Hidden Immigrants," by Elda Isabel Garcia White. In this January 4, 1998 letter, the writer laments how students of Portuguese heritage are deprived from the opportunity to study Portuguese in many of our school systems for lack of course offerings. Even with today's preoccupation with inclusion and diversity, the Portuguese are, more often than not, excluded. Dad was proud to be American but still proud to be of Portuguese descent, and encouraged me to pursue and promote my heritage. It was touching to me to see this clipping among his things, not *because* I became involved in the Portuguese community, but well *before* I became involved.

Mention has been made more than once, that Dad was a self-educated man. The college dictionary I gave him one Christmas was not only well-thumbed but dogeared. Whenever he came upon a new word, usually while reading but occasionally while listening, he would rush to look it up. Among his papers I found a ruled tablet with a letter of the alphabet written at the top of each sheet of paper to record his new words. Each entry was alphabetically arranged in his beautiful penmanship, written in syllables and diacritical marks, with the definition of each. He truly studied the dictionary and the thesaurus as well, following through with Mr. Gus Olson's lessons in vocabulary from junior high school.

At a couple of points in the book, mention is made of Dad's artistic ability, particularly in drawings that he attempted though only on occasion. What he did and could use every day was his most beautiful handwriting. He had the most fluid and graceful script, which I could never replicate to forge his signature on my occasional deficient school paper. Two of the skills of which he was most proud, that were diminished by Parkinson's Disease, were his speech articulation and his handwriting. Nevertheless, he would not let the disease define him. He wisely worked as long as he could to record his experiences, thoughts, and feelings for us to contemplate long after he was gone leaving with us a truly rich legacy indeed.

When I began this project, there was no doubt that it would be a labor of love, but I also felt it would be a journey to rediscover my father as the whole man he was, as each scrap of paper and each photo fell into its place. Throughout it all, I laughed and I cried with him, feeling his hand on my shoulder the entire time.

Addenda:
Tributes, Letters, and Notes

TRIBUTE

Not one to seek praise, Dad was surprised and touched to receive this unsolicited recognition in the mail one day. This personal tribute was hand created by an acquaintance who was impressed by Dad's contributions in the local newspaper. It was sent by Mr. Joseph M. Mattias, a local sign painter, who did business under the name JOMA at 27 Edward Street, Coventry, Rhode Island.

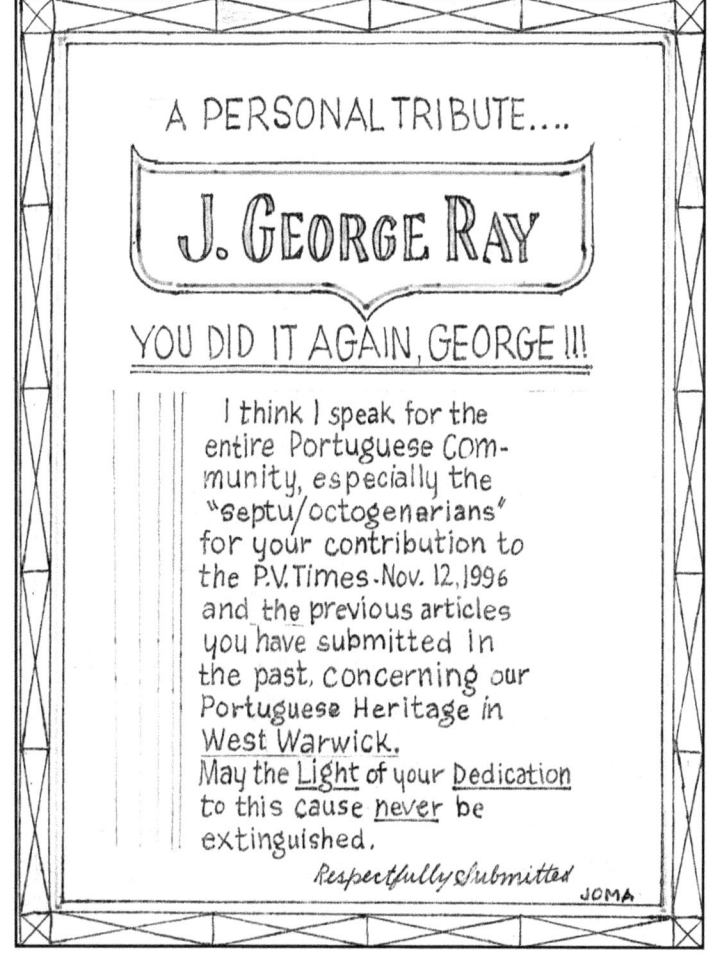

LETTERS

From Patty Gibney, wife of Frank Gibney, RE: Article "Frank Gibney: A gifted teacher remembered over the years."

February 10, 1997

Dear Joe,

It was very good of you to call Frank and to remember him so kindly.

I asked him about those stories you told me. He recalled you and the 35 boys and the poetry and pooning a kid with a piece of chalk. He got a big laugh out of it. Just thinking about it brought back the good old days of teaching "good kids." No matter how noisy and active they were, they were "good-hearted." That's probably because they knew they were expected to be respectful at home and at school, too.

Frank is on home care–and this morning he told the nurse about your call and proceeded to recite the poetry to her. She thought he should put it on tape.

He really enjoyed his male classes. Teaching all those boys to love the classics and poetry was a challenge. I think the fact that Frank loved sports and was a big tall man helped to convince you boys that it was ok to be a jock and still love poetry. He regrets that he isn't able to play golf but he and his pal, Jimmy Kane ride around Buttonwoods visiting the neighbors in Jim's golf cart...

The pictures enclosed are the best I can do. I understand the Champlin Library in the old newspaper section has old sports pictures of Frank.

Frank will be entertaining me with quotes from "Romeo and Juliet," "Casey at the Bat," "Evangeline," his favorite, now that you've mentioned and reminded him of it.

Please remember us to Doris (Kelly)–always a very nice lady–and give my love to Amby Smith, a classmate of mine. Thank you for asking about Frank and he wishes you health and happiness in the coming year.

Sincerely,
Patty Gibney

March 20, 1997

Dear Joe,

A neighbor brought the Times to our daughter, Alice, with Frank's write-up in the paper. I can't find a store that sells it around here.

No matter. I've run off copies of it. Frank was thrilled and so was Alice with not only the very kind write-up but that it included the pictures. It was great! I thank you for remembering him. He'll be 88 April 15th–so you provided a lovely gift to him.

Sincerely,
Patty Gibney
(Note: Daughter Alice Gibney has served as RI Superior Court Judge since 1984)

NOTES

From Peter Kelly, son of John Kelly RE: Letters to the Editor: "Teachers did make a huge difference."

December 15, 1995

Dear Mr. Ray,

A while ago, my mother showed me a copy of your fine letter praising my father and Gus Olson. She asked me to let you know that your kind words meant very much to her (and the rest of our family).

Thank you and best wishes for a happy Christmas.

Peter Kelly

From Doris E. Kelly, wife of John Kelly

January 27, 1996

All I can say, Joseph –

You are a sweetheart. I'm adopting you as my third son.

Would you mind if I call you when Pete and wife, Lori, are visiting? I would like to consummate this friendship. We'll tip a glass of wine. That is, if you indulge, Joseph.

Incidentally, we all agreed you are quite handsome. Along with being a beautiful person inside. Your parents must be very proud.

Too bad John had to leave us. He would be so proud of you.

Thank you, Joseph, for caring. "God Bless"

Affectionately,
Doris E. Kelly

February, 1997

Greetings, Joseph –

I enjoyed reading your poems, especially "My Mother's Daughter." I will frame it and put it on my wall. Thank you, Joseph.

Sincerely,
Doris E. Kelly

P.S. Joseph—I was impressed with your drawing of The Ledge on Wakefield Street. You are a very talented gentleman. "God Bless"

1997

A rose for you, Joseph.

Thank you most sincerely for your loyalty and respect for John. I am proud to be your friend.

Affectionately,
Doris E. Kelly

P.S. When John was a teacher at Jr. High, the students presented him with these lovely bookends. That was 47 years ago or 49. I can't think of anyone more deserving of this gift, Joseph. I'm sure John would agree. Best of luck to you and your family—
God Bless, Doris E. K.

From Tara Finlay, Waitress Extraordinaire, The Villa at St. Antoine's

c. 2010

DEAR GEORGE,

THANKS FOR BEING BRAVE.
THANKS FOR CARING ABOUT EVERYONE.
THANKS FOR TAKING YOUR TIME TO TELL ME WHAT TOOK YOU SO LONG TO LEARN.
THANKS FOR YOUR JOKES, TOO.

From Roberta Faria, daughter of John "Saulty" Amaral RE: Article "John 'Saulty' Amaral: the last of the Lippitt Tigers"

September 14, 1997

Mr. Ray,

The article you prepared featuring my dad, Saulty, in the Kent County Daily Times, has given me and my family much joy and comfort. Friends and relatives have mentioned your tribute to him. You worked many hours, I am certain, to get the story "just right" but mostly I appreciate the time you shared during your visit with me to reminisce. All the articles you prepare bring a warm spot to our hearts here in "the Valley." Many thanks to you and a prayer of thanksgiving for your kindness are sent with this note. God bless you!

Sincerely,
Bobbie

From Leslie Ray, Niece and Daughter of Tommy Ray

April 4, 2023

My Uncle George always made me smile! I was always amazed at the way he could put his thoughts and words on paper in such a poetic way. I remember being proud of the articles published in the local paper and on display at Evelyn's restaurant. I actually have one of his poems on my bulletin board at work now that had especially touched me.

He always had a twinkle in his eyes reminding me a lot of my dad. I was fortunate to have breakfast with the two of them when Uncle George was at the assisted living facility. He would enjoy showing me his works and pictures! I feel grateful for that time. He will always be missed!

From Erin Lee Maher, Grand-niece and daughter of Leslie Ray

June 28, 2023

Uncle George would come to Evelyn's to eat once in a while when I worked there. I can remember waiting on him and at what table at the Villa. He was always so nice to me. I was pretty young. I always remember him as just a sweet man.

From Gail Ray Coken, Niece and daughter of Tommy Ray

June 29, 2023

I loved spending time with Uncle George. I got to see him a lot when we lived around the corner on Harris Avenue.

One of the things I remember was that when I was a child, he treated me like a loved niece...when I was an adult, he treated me with respect for my accomplishments at work and my opinion! His smile and laugh were a joy.

From Paul Dressel, Nephew/Godson and son of Eileen Furtado Dressel

July 1, 2023

Uncle George

My Uncle George, my Godfather, my Padrinho taught me many things. Most often without intention I suspect, as respected elders influence the youngsters in their orbit.

Uncle George was in many ways a "working man's Renaissance man." It seemed he had the ability to take from his many life experiences ideas that would advance his thinking, always seeking a greater understanding of life and self-expression.

He was a personal "hero." I stood in awe watching him fix an electrical connection with speed and precision. I later found out the painting in my childhood room of a sleeping babe set upon by candle toting pixies, the springboard for many a dream and daydream, was painted by him. He became a folk art hero.

In later years as he offered self-study techniques and observations of life, we would engage in a sort of Socratic banter which I think we both enjoyed.

Uncle George had great recall and would share many stories with a flair of humor and a touch of poignancy. Hearing his recollections of my Avô (my maternal grandfather, Luiz Furtado) were especially welcome. Raconteur. Hero.

He also worked with words. Paragraphs became stories, thoughts became stanzas. He told tales of the old neighborhood, the characters there, and the shared experiences of many in "The Valley." His ventures into poetry yielded a more personal view. Wearing yet another hat, a man of letters.

My Uncle George: Godfather, Padrinho, Renaissance Man, Hero.

MILITARY PROFILE
T/SGT JOSEPH RAY, U.S. ARMY

Joseph Ray, reported for induction into the U.S. Army on March 3, 1943 and was processed at Fort Devens, Massachusetts. He was transported by troop train to Camp Shelby, Mississippi for seventeen weeks of basic training and then, was assigned to the 623rd Light Equipment Engineering Company as an automotive mechanic.

He traveled with his company to the staging area in Camp Shanks, New York from where he departed aboard the "Santa Barbara" to Liverpool, England on 9 January, 1944.

On June 21, 1944, the company crossed the English Channel and landed in Normandy on Omaha Beach.

He participated in campaigns in Normandy, Northern France, Rhineland, Ardennes, and Central Europe during which no fewer than forty-one motor marches are documented. Following the Armistice with Japan on August 12, 1945, the unit was returned stateside aboard the USS General Harry Taylor arriving on 13 September 1945 at Camp Shanks, New York.

T/SGT Ray was honorably discharged on October 25, 1945 at Fort Devens, Massachusetts and awarded the Good Conduct Medal and European African Middle Eastern Theatre Campaign Ribbon.

Contributions Published In The Kent County Daily Times

(Previously *Pawtuxet Valley Daily Times*)

SENIORS COLUMN: AMBY SMITH, SENIOR SCENE EDITOR

In Memory of Joe King, "Joe King: 35 years after death, he's still admired," May 10, 1995.

On Francis "Hurricane" Carley, "Old photograph stirs memories of a bygone baseball era," Jan. 23, 1996.

On Thornton's Theater and Jim Lamb Orchestra, "There was a time when the Pawtuxet Valley throbbed with entertainment," Feb. 20, 1996.

On the Lace Trade, "Remembering the many artisans who helped create prosperity in the Valley," Jul. 30, 1996.

On the Hindenburg passing over the Valley, "Hindenburg memories live on," May 2, 1996.

On Ralph Caldamone, "Ralph the Barber's community roots run deep."

On the Doucette Lot Boys, "Memories of boyhood days long gone by," Oct. 15, 1996.

On St. Anthony's Holy Name Society, "Valley men celebrate reunion at Narragansett retreat home," Oct. 1996.

On the Hurricane of '38, "Memories of the monster they called "No-Name Hurricane," Sep. 3, 1996.

On Sgt. George Luz in WWII, "They speak softly of our debt to them," Dec. 31, 1996.

On Educator John Kelly, "In memory of a man who stood tall in our community," Feb. 4, 1997.

On Plane Crash and Meddy Payette

On John Amaral, "John "Saulty" Amaral: the last of the Lippett Tigers," May 20, 1997.

On Educator Frank Gibney, "Frank Gibney: A gifted teacher remembered over the years," Mar. 18, 1997.

Quoted in: The Valley loses a fine man and great teacher in Frank Gibney, Nov. 18, 1997.

LETTERS TO THE EDITOR: JOSEPH G. RAY

Introspective of Holocaust

"Let's do what has to be done."

Teachers did make a huge difference, Jan 6, 1995

The Ledge and PePe Laroche, Jan. 19, 1995

Memorial deserves respect, Feb. 2, 1996

Time is a chronology of human civilization, Apr. 9, 1997

Do I have assurance of clean gasoline?, Jun. 6, 1997

POETRY CORNER

"A commentary on monetary."

"Ambulating at Sunrise."

"My Buffalo Nickel And The Man In The Hat," Nov. 18, 1998.

"Love Letters Never Sent," Jan. 1, 1999.

"My Mother's Daughter," Feb. 25, 1999.

Shadow in Decline, Apr. 8, 1999.

Endnotes

i State of Rhode Island and Providence Plantations, Division of Vital Statistics, Dept. of Health

ii Ancestry.com

iii Rey Name Meaning: Spanish Galician and French (Occitan): from Spanish and Old French rey 'king' (from Latin rex genitive regis) which may have denoted someone in the service of a king or it may have been from the title of someone in a brotherhood or a nickname for someone who behaved in a regal fashion or who had earned the title in some contest of skill or by presiding over festivities... Source: https://www.ancestry.com/name-origin?surname=rey

iv *Alcunha*: Portuguese for nickname, https://www.collinsdictionary.com/dictionary/english-portuguese/nickname

v Per conversation with Lucy Riccio Ray, widow of John Ray, January, 2000.

vi Lippitt is known as a Portuguese neighborhood, as large numbers of Portuguese immigrants settled in this area in the 1890s and still occupy the area today. Their Feast of the Holy Ghost, put on every year in September, is known throughout the state and draws a large following. http://www.milltowndocumentary.org/villages/

vii Porto Editora – *corisco* no Dicionário infopédia da Língua Portuguesa [em linha]. Porto: Porto Editora. [consult. 2023-06-25 18:30:55]. Disponível em https://www.infopedia.pt/dicionarios/lingua-portuguesa/corisco

viii Encyclopedia of Azorean Culture: http://www.culturacores.azores.gov.pt/ea/pesquisa/Default.aspx? id=8535

ix Located at Hillsgrove State Airport, now the Rhode Island T. F. Green International Airport in Warwick, RI x From conversations with Dad, it was always my impression that none of the Ray siblings were allowed to stay in school past their sixteenth birthday. Like many in Azorean immigrant families, the children were expected to stay in school only up until the mandatory requirement so they could begin working to help support the family.

xi Finding his Army uniform showed a jacket size of 32 and pants waist of 31 inches.

xii The landing craft, tank (or tank landing craft) was an amphibious assault craft for landing tanks on beachheads. They were initially developed by the British Royal Navy and later by the United States Navy during World War II in a series of versions. Initially known as the "tank landing craft" (TLC) by the British, they later adopted the U.S. nomenclature "landing craft, tank" (LCT). https://en.wikipedia.org/wiki/Landing_craft_tank

xiii Extracts of Morning Reports, "The History of the 623rd Engineer Light Equipment Company," report states that the LCT was loaded at 1200 and left port at 1500 arriving in France at 1600 on June 21, 1944.

xiv Extracts of Morning Reports, "The History of the 623rd Engineer Light Equipment Company," states moved into bivouac area near Travieres, France at 2100 hrs.

xv Sulzberger, C. L., The American Heritage Picture History of World War II, 1966, p. 511.

xvi My father mentioned that he had taken photos of some of these scenes in the concentration camp that he sent home. Unfortunately, a family member spilled a bottle of ink on them ruining them so they were destroyed.

xvii **Lipizzaner**, also spelled **Lippizaner**, also called **Lipizzan**, breed of horse that derived its name from the Austrian imperial stud at Lipizza, near Trieste, formerly a part of the Austro-Hungarian Empire. The founding of the breed dates to 1580, and detailed breeding records date from 1700. The ancestry is Spanish, Arabian, and Berber. (Encyclopedia Britannica, https://www.britannica.com/animal/Lipizzaner)

xviii Author's Note: Although not his intention, I believe that my father would have been pleased to see his words preserved in print. He told me that he wanted to commit his experiences in writing so that his grandsons would learn about and understand the significance of that time.

xix Charles, Roland W., "Santa Barbara," Troopships of World War II, The Army Transportation Association, Washington, D.C., 1947, p. 243.

End Notes

xx Koerner, CPT Paul C., "The History of 623rd Engineer Light Equipment Company, World War II," Camp Gruber, OK, 27 Nov 1945.

xxi Koerner, CPT Paul C., "The History of 623rd Engineer Light Equipment Company, World War II," Camp Gruber, OK, 27 Nov 1945.

xxii Koerner, CPT Paul C., "The History of 623rd Engineer Light Equipment Company, World War II," Camp Gruber, OK, 27 Nov 1945.

xxiii Cross of Honor of the German Mother, https://en.m.wikipedia.org/wiki/Cross_of_Honour_of_the_German_Mother

xxv Koerner, CPT Paul C., "The History of 623rd Engineer Light Equipment Company, World War II," Camp Gruber, OK, 27 Nov 1945.

xxv New England Historical Society, https://newenglandhistoricalsociety.com/hurricane-carol-deadly-name-retired/

xxvi "How much does a piano weigh?" https://www.moving.com/tips/how-much-does-a-piano-weigh/

xxvii Truman, Harold G., and Edward F. Walker, Eds., Leavers Lace: A Hand Book of the American Leavers Lace Industry, (Prepared under the direction of Professor Vittoria Rosatto, Head of the Department of Design and Weaving, Lowell Textile Institute, Lowell, MA from a study made by Professor Edward L Golec and George G. Armstrong, Jr., July 1948), Providence, RI 1949, p. 3. https://www2.cs.arizona.edu/patterns/weaving/books/rv_ll_01.pdf

xxviii Leavers machine, https://en.m.wikipedia.org/wiki/Leavers_machine#Description

xxix Spalding, John, "Dry Lubrication of Textile Machines," United States Patent Office, 1928, https://patentimages.storage.googleapis.com/pdfs/US1694148.pdf

xxx Greige is an unfinished woven or knitted fabric that hasn't been bleached or dyed. It can be used for upholstery, window treatments, clothes and more. https://www.zsfabrics.com/store/c319/Greige_Fabric.html

xxxi Caroline Randell Exquisite Lingerie, "How is Leavers Lace Created?", https://www.carolinerandell.co.uk/blogs/news/a-guide-to-leavers-lace

xxxii Valley Lace Company was owned by Weiner Laces, Inc. and incorporated as a Domestic Profit Corporation in the State of Rhode Island on November 29, 1933. https://business.sos.ri.gov/CorpWeb/CorpSearch/CorpSummary.aspx?FEIN=000013993&SEARCH_TYPE=1

xxxiii Constitution of the Amalgamated Lace Operatives of America, Lever Section, 1961, Article IV, Section 1, p. 7.

xxxiv Constitution of the Amalgamated Lace Operatives of America, Lever Section, 1961, Article IV, Section 1, p. 6.

xxxv Constitution of the Amalgamated Lace Operatives of America, Lever Section, 1961, Article IV, Section 5, p. 7.

xxxvi Fraley, Marie R., "Growing Up Portuguese in the Lace Trade of the Pawtuxet Valley," Keynote Address at Portuguese Honors at Rhode Island College, Unpublished, 2018.

xxxvii https://www.westwarwickfirefighters.org/history.html

xxxviii Report of the Technical Investigation of The Station Nightclub Fire, https://www.govinfo.gov/content/pkg/GOVPUB-C13-a3976672cebdbe486ff4ba4c416159be/pdf/GOVPUB-C13-a3976672cebdbe486ff4ba4c416159be.pdf

xxxix The Station Nightclub Fire, https://en.m.wikipedia.org/wiki/The_Station_nightclub_fire

xl Ambrose Smith, 1917-2005, was a sports editor and Vice President of the *Pawtucket Valley Daily Times* (later the *Kent County Daily Times*), for which he served for forty-two years. A native of West Warwick, RI, he served his community and state for many years as a leading exponent of youth programs. He became one of the most sought after speakers in Rhode Island, and received numerous honors. Source: https://riheritage-halloffame.com/Ambrose-Smith/

References

Belcher, Genevieve. Villages, A Brief History of West Warwick's Villages. Milltown, 2016. http://www.milltowndocumentary.org/villages/

Charles, Roland W. Troopships of World War II. The Army Transportation Association. Washington, D.C., 1947.

Constitution of the Amalgamated Lace Operatives of American, Lever Section. 1961.

Fragoeiro, António. "Jorge Rei—Relato e Memórias de Um Lusodescendente." Revista Portuguesa de História Militar—Dossier: Portugal no Contexto da Segunda Guerra Mundial, 1939-1945. Lisboa. ISSN 2795-4323. Ano III, nº 4 (Junho 2023); https://doi.org/10.56092/CLKK2486

Fraley, Marie R. "Growing Up Portuguese in the Lace Trade of the Pawtuxet Valley." Keynote Address at Portuguese Honors at Rhode Island College. Unpublished. April 23, 2018.

Golec, Edward Lucian, George Gordon Armstrong, Vittoria Rosatto, and American Lace Manufacturers Association. 1950. *Leavers Lace: A Hand Book of the American Leavers Lace Industry*. Providence.

Grosshandler, William, Nelson Bryner, Daniel Madrzykowski, Kenneth Kuntz. Report of the Technical Investigation of The Station Nightclub, National Institute of Standards and Technology. U.S. Department of Commerce. v.1. 2005.

"Historic and Architectural Resources of Scituate, Rhode Island: A Preliminary Report." Rhode Island Historical and Preservation Commission. Providence. 1987.

"Historic and Architectural Resources of West Warwick, Rhode Island: A Preliminary Report." Rhode Island Historical and Preservation Commission. Providence. May, 1980.

Koerner, CPT Paul C. "The History of 623rd Engineer Light Equipment Company, World War II." Camp Gruber, OK. 27 Nov 1945.

Porto Editora, Dicionário infopédia da Língua Portuguesa [em linha]. Porto: Porto Editora. [consult. 2023-06-25 18:30:55]. Disponível em https://www.infopedia.pt/dicionarios/lingua-portuguesa/corisco

Ray, Joseph George, interview by Dulce Maria Scott, August 25, 2011.

Spalding, John. "Dry Lubrication of Textile Machines." United States Patent Office. 1928.

Acknowledgments

We all stand on someone else's shoulders. For me, there could not be broader nor stronger shoulders than that of my father, Joseph George Ray, who inspired me in so many ways throughout my life. In compiling his works, photos, and notes for this book, I felt a collaboration with him that was not only a bittersweet challenge but a gift. My thanks to him are without end.

At times in life, if we are fortunate, a person enters at just the right time and place to walk a path with us to accomplish goals difficult to meet alone. When Professor Silvia Oliveira arrived at Rhode Island College to teach Portuguese and to work with the Institute for Portuguese and Lusophone World Studies, she filled a much-needed vacuum in scholarship, mentorship, and professionalism. Because of her expertise and wise advocacy, the Portuguese Studies Program at Rhode Island College has flourished and the Institute for Portuguese and Lusophone World Studies has thrived under her directorship. I am not only deeply grateful for her partnership over the years that we worked together, but for her encouragement, her careful reading and editorial advice, her insightful observations in the Foreword, and her general support in helping me to elevate the work of this book to a higher level.

To former General Treasurer Paul Tavares, I extend my heartfelt thanks for contributing to the Foreword in this text. Your endorsement, not only as a highly respected figure in the Portuguese community but also as a son of immigrants walking a similar path as my father's, is much valued and appreciated. Thank you for always being supportive of the many projects in which I enlisted your help throughout the years. You never said, "No."

To António Fragoeiro, researcher of Portuguese military history, thank you for prompting my participation in your collaborative website, "Portugal, 1939–1945," By contributing the military profiles of my father and uncles, you spurred me on to organizing the material for his book. Thank you for honoring his service in the featured article of the "Revista Portuguesa de História Militar" and supporting his story.

To Dr. Dulce Maria Scott, I extend my thanks for including my father's story in her scholarly work, for contributing her insights of the Portuguese American experience, and for her expertise.

To Janie Jessee, publisher at Jan-Carol Publishing, Inc., and her staff, many thanks for your patience and expert advice in bringing this dream of mine to reality. Thank you, especially for recognizing that this is a "work of the heart" worthy of print.

Finally, but most importantly, I reserve my most profound thanks for my family: to all who loved my father and contributed their thoughts in writing; to my sons for their unflagging encouragement; to my daughter-in-law, Jennifer, daughter of my heart, who designed the meaningful and beautiful cover art that captured the essence of a life well-lived; and to my granddaughter, Michelle, for whom I hope my father's legacy will one day have special meaning in the future.

Most of all, and from the bottom of my heart, I am eternally grateful to my husband, Dave, my life partner for over fifty years. He never fails to support me in anything I undertake no matter how much it costs him. Amid health challenges this year, he has been my rock, as always, in helping me finalize this much-desired tribute to a man we both loved.

MARIE RAY FRALEY

The granddaughter of Azorean immigrants from the island of *São Miguel*, Marie Fraley was born, raised and educated in the small Portuguese parish of St. Anthony's in Riverpoint, Rhode Island. Although all four grandparents immigrated to the United States at the turn of the century, learning the Portuguese language was never encouraged by the family so strong was the desire for assimilation into American society at that time.

She was the first in the family to attain a college education, from the University of Rhode Island with a B.A. (1972) and a M.S. (1974) in Speech-language Pathology. She worked with language disabled children in Providence and Cumberland School Districts for over 20 years. She also pursued graduate study in Linguistics at Brown University and holds a certificate in Non-Profit Studies from Rhode Island College.

Following retirement, curiosity about her own family history led her to the island of *São Miguel* and the *Biblioteca Pública E Arquivo de Ponta Delgada* where she not only traced her family tree but met long-lost family. Eager to learn more, she enrolled in Portuguese classes at Rhode Island College where she helped lead a community movement to establish the Institute for Portuguese and Lusophone World Studies, retiring as Director in December, 2018.

She served on the RI Day of Portugal Committee from 2004 in various roles including President (2008), Vice-President, Public Relations Chair, and Fundraising Chair and served several terms on the Board of Directors. She helped to return the state Day of

Portugal celebrations to the capital city of Providence in 2007 which eventually culminated in a Portuguese-themed *WaterFire*, jointly hosted by RI Day of Portugal and Rhode Island College Institute for Portuguese and Lusophone World Studies in 2017. She was honored to serve as the RI Day of Portugal Parade Grand Marshal for 2020-2021.

A Charter Member of PALCUS since 2003, she served on the Board of Directors representing Rhode Island from 2007 until 2021 in various capacities of Vice-Chair, Secretary, Managing Director, Gala Chair, and By-Laws Committee Chair. She was the architect and national director of the campaign, Make Portuguese Count™ in the 2020 U.S. Census that oversaw the participation of 220 affiliated Portuguese-American organizations and 75 area captains in the write-in national campaign.

Now permanently retired, Marie and her husband of 50 years, David (whose support has been indispensable), divide their time between the Midwest and New England. They are the proud parents of John M. Fraley of Massachusetts and Dr. Benjamin Fraley of Wisconsin and grandparents of Michelle Anne.

www.ingramcontent.com/pod-product-compliance
Lightning Source LLC
Chambersburg PA
CBHW080603170426
43196CB00017B/2883